CW00818806

ENGLISH NARRATIVE POEMS

WITH AN INTRODUCTION
BY
SIR HENRY NEWBOLT, M.A., D.Litt.

LONDON
EDWARD ARNOLD & CO.

Made in Great Britain. Printed at the St Ann's Press
Timperley, Altrincham

CONTENTS

INTRODUCTION

By SIR HENRY NEWBOLT

THE art of narrative is commonly thought to be no special
gift ; but there are not, in fact, many of us who can bring even
an anecdote to full effect or give a clear account of a scene or
a conversation. In *Much Ado about Nothing* we are all hit
off in a single passing phrase. " I tell this tale vilely," says
Borachio in the middle of his treacherous story ; and he
goes back hastily to lay the bit of foundation he had omitted.
Even among professed story-tellers the scale of narrative
power is steeply graduated. Some, with abundant fore-
thought and scholarship, only succeed in boring us ;
others, as Stevenson said of Dumas, have a style with every
fault, but yet inimitably right. Meredith is terse to the verge
of obscurity, De Morgan lengthy almost to garrulousness ;
yet both hold the reader as a hundred and one more careful
writers fail to do. They can both tell a story : it comes
natural to them, and therefore to their audience.

Among poets the narrative gift is one of the rarest of all.
There are perhaps several reasons for this. The essentially
poetic moods are the lyric and the dramatic : in them the
effort of expression is more instinctive, and the material
more easily dealt with. A story naturally contains a larger
admixture of prosaic stuff ; and it demands of the writer
a special attitude. He cannot simply sing to himself and
please by being overheard ; nor can he, like the dramatist,
lose and find himself in the characters which he creates
to act his passions. He has to tell of persons in whom hardly
anything of himself is reproduced, and of events in which

he himself bears no part ; often he must be simply a reporter,
and always he must be present with his audience. This
special attitude may possibly be acquired by taking thought,
but it is difficult to believe so, when we look at the number
and respectability of the failures. The poetical museum is
full of narrative poems—mostly epics of the kind which,
as Gaston Paris said, " have the misfortune not to exist."
Their subject-matter may be partly in fault, but it seems
that no subject is impossible to the born teller of stories :
his gift has always been irresistible. Still, there may be
limits to his scope or his ambition. To tell the story of a
whole people, and transpose it from the human to the heroic
scale, is a task for a giant, and not all poets are giants.
The number of those who would attempt anything of the
kind grows steadily smaller, though the present state of
the world offers them material in plenty.

The poets of the nineteenth century were cautious in this
respect : they were many of them drawn to the telling of
stories, but they knew better than to overtask their powers
in the attempt to build the loftiest towers of poetry. In a
representative selection from their work you will find lengths
of epic masonry, but never the whole dim-rich city with
the soul of a people built into its streets and battlements
and palaces. Tennyson knew as well as any man what is
an epic, and it would be of surpassing interest to
question how he came to write his early poem " Morte
d'Arthur " in the form of a fragment, and upon what
considerations he followed up this first success by dealing
with the Arthurian cycle not as one story, but as a series
strung upon an allegory. The later plan was a distortion
of Malory's : the former inspiration was something very
different—a " faint Homeric echo," Tennyson himself calls it.

In " Sohrab and Rustum " there are echoes too : the
fighting is Homeric, and the manners, and above all the
similes. The imitation—by which is meant the adaptation

of existing methods—is clearly conscious, but it is in no way mechanical : the fine rhythm, the sense of romance, and the restrained dramatic power are all the unique contribution of Matthew Arnold, a poet giving not of his labour or ingenuity, but of his abundant personal pleasure. A comparison of his poem with " Morte d'Arthur " is interesting. Tennyson is inspired by his original, Malory, follows him or adds to him with most delicate art, and makes a new thing out of the old by the intensity of his visionary mood. Arnold goes further afield, and draws from more varied sources ; also the cadences which mark his mood owe less to any predecessor that we recognise. He has the advantage, too, of knowing the scope of his work from the beginning : it is an epic in little, not a fragment, and the actors in it have a type of character that seems nearer to historical humanity than the types of the Tennysonian romance of chivalry. Yet, like Arthur and Bedivere, they seem to be too remote from us for a true epic : the race from which they come was not " ta'en from the common earth," but from the dust of literature ; their beauty, exquisite as it is, reminds us rather of illuminated manuscripts than of the battlefields of France.

Longfellow studied the same problem, and attempted it under somewhat the same limitations, when he wrote " Hiawatha." He desired to preserve the character and traditions of a dying race ; and, since it was in the main a childish race with hardly any recorded history, his poem became a kind of child's epic, a set of folk-tales gathered round a typical hero-chief. Its excellence is due to the sympathetic treatment and to the charm of Longfellow's own temperament ; its defects are the brevity and monotony of the metre, and the inevitable doubt of the claim to human reality. The character attributed to a nation by one wholly alien in race and civilization is certainly attractive and poetical ; but it fails to move us, because it reminds

A*

us once more rather of myth than of mankind as we know it.

Scott succeeded better. His "Lord of the Isles" has a poor plot and some tedious intervals ; its line is as brief and monotonous as Longfellow's, and less original ; but he has the great excellence of undoubted truth. We neither know nor care much about the historical accuracy of his characters : we have an absolute security that they and their passions live, because we feel in them the warm and generous life of Scott himself. He gives us beyond question the manners and feelings of a nation and an age, his own nation and his own age, that is ; and, while we retain our sympathy with them so long will his epical poems continue to stir us. In the campaigns of to-day they are found to be good reading.

Distinct from all these is the Tale, properly so-called, the story in verse whose aim is not to re-create or transfigure the life of a people, a generation or a hero, but to entertain us with a narrative where the events and individuals, whether ordinary or extraordinary, are yet in the scale of common life. Chaucer is, of course, the supreme example of this art in our own language ; his tales are not only told with perfect skill, they are enriched with a wonderful study of English character, and they have in a high degree the poetical merit of revealing to us Chaucer himself, in his humour and philosophy as he lived. Of those who have followed him, Crabbe is by common consent the nearest in method and temperament : he has the eye for character, and the instinct for its effect on the events of the story ; he can, it is true, be tedious or prosaic at times, but he is a fine teller of tales, and his philosophy appears now and then in passages markedly ironic, moralistic or genial, and sometimes in a line or two of deep poetical beauty.

Crabbe's worst fault was the lingering habit of the conventional eighteenth-century style. Wordsworth's busi-

ness, as we know, was to free English poetry from the rags
of that once fashionable brocade. He was not a pure story-
teller, as Crabbe was, but he shared his love of character,
and brought to the observation of it a more profound insight.
The story of " Michael " is not well proportioned—it begins
with a loving perfection of draughtsmanship that is almost
mocked by the abruptness of the work towards the end.
But its main object is attained : the character of a man and
a remote country life could not be more admirably set forth
—though the art is always intentional, it proceeds from a
sincerity which makes a false tone or an irrelevant personal
touch impossible.

Wordsworth had other aims in view than the telling of
tales ; he had little of the Chaucerian gift ; but a later
generation saw it reappear in William Morris. So great was
this poet's admiration for Chaucer that in the Envoi to the
" Earthly Paradise " he sends his book to him as the greeting
of a humble pupil, content to forgo fame if only he can
win the approval of his beloved master. Yet even the stories
in those four volumes are by no means all Chaucerian :
the " Lovers of Gudrun " is a saga, and the Greek stories,
though treated with all Chaucer's romance, are not, like
his " Troilus," transposed into the key of contemporary
English life. "Atalanta's Race " is an interesting example
of the likeness and difference. The vision of Venus, and the
invocation to her, are reminiscent ; but the pictorial quality
is distinctive, and so is the lyrical rise in tone which comes
with almost a dramatic effect at the end of the story. It
is evident that Keats in his " Eve of St. Agnes " had already
given just these two characters, of the lyrical and the
pictorial, to the new mediævalism : but the influence of
his poetry upon Morris is negligible when set beside the
latter's own fertile vitality. The " Mazeppa " of Byron
and the " Pheidippides " of Browning carry us a step further
into the region of feeling where the story becomes frankly

the dramatic lyric. Browning's studies in this form of poetry are, of course, far more interesting than Byron's; but they led him further and further from true narrative into a world where the imagination is stirred and satisfied by a situation and a character, without scenery, description, plot, or even a personal name. " Pheidippides " and " Hervé Riel " are stories still, admirably imagined and sustained; but it can never be anything but difficult to keep a tale of such a length at so high a pitch of intensity, without falsifying, or stumbling over, some more humdrum details. It was in the achievement of this difficult feat that the writers of the old ballads showed unrivalled power: the form of their convention has a magic property, and enabled them to mingle verses of epic splendour with others of harmless necessary flatness or of exquisite and convincing commonplace. Coleridge chose a ballad form for his tale of the "Ancient Mariner," and showed that the magic was one which had not lost its efficacy, but could work wonders even in a self-conscious age and for the sake of an avowed experiment. It seems more than possible that the ballad story has a long and wider life before it yet: the poet who can tell his tale naturally in this form will avoid elaboration on the one hand and empty simplicity on the other; his lyrical mood will add to his power without depriving him of the use of humour; he may mark character, personal or national, and he may touch in a supreme moment the deepest chords of the heart.

I.—TENNYSON

MORTE D'ARTHUR

So all day long the noise of battle roll'd
Among the mountains by the winter sea;
Until King Arthur's table, man by man,
Had fallen in Lyonnesse about their Lord,
King Arthur: then, because his wound was deep,
The bold Sir Bedivere uplifted him,
Sir Bedivere, the last of all his knights,
And bore him to a chapel nigh the field,
A broken chancel with a broken cross,
That stood on a dark strait of barren land.   10
On one side lay the Ocean, and on one
Lay a great water, and the moon was full.
   Then spake King Arthur to Sir Bedivere:
"The sequel of to-day unsolders all
The goodliest fellowship of famous knights
Whereof this world holds record. Such a sleep
They sleep—the men I loved. I think that we
Shall never more, at any future time,
Delight our souls with talk of knightly deeds,
Walking about the gardens and the halls   20
Of Camelot, as in the days that were.
I perish by this people which I made,—
Tho' Merlin sware that I should come again
To rule once more—but let what will be, be,
I am so deeply smitten thro' the helm
That without help I cannot last till morn.
Thou therefore take my brand Excalibur,

7

Which was my pride : for thou rememberest how
In those old days, one summer noon, an arm
Rose up from out the bosom of the lake,   30
Clothed in white samite, mystic, wonderful,
Holding the sword—and how I row'd across
And took it, and have worn it, like a king :
And, wheresoever I am sung or told
In aftertime, this also shall be known :
But now delay not : take Excalibur,
And fling him far into the middle mere :
Watch what thou seest, and lightly bring me word."

    To him replied the bold Sir Bedivere :
" It is not meet, Sir King, to leave thee thus,   40
Aidless, alone, and smitten thro' the helm.
A little thing may harm a wounded man.
Yet I thy hest will all perform at full,
Watch what I see, and lightly bring thee word."

    So saying, from the ruin'd shrine he stept
And in the moon athwart the place of tombs,
Where lay the mighty bones of ancient men,
Old knights, and over them the sea-wind sang
Shrill, chill, with flakes of foam. He, stepping down
By zig-zag paths, and juts of pointed rock,   50
Came on the shining levels of the lake.

    There drew he forth the brand Excalibur,
And o'er him, drawing it, the winter moon,
Brightening the skirts of a long cloud, ran forth
And sparkled keen with frost against the hilt :
For all the haft twinkled with diamond sparks,
Myriads of topaz-lights, and jacinth-work
Of subtlest jewellery. He gazed so long
That both his eyes were dazzled, as he stood,
This way and that dividing the swift mind,   60
In act to throw : but at the last it seem'd
Better to leave Excalibur conceal'd

There in the many-knotted waterflags,
That whistled stiff and dry about the marge.
So strode he back slow to the wounded King.
  Then spake King Arthur to Sir Bedivere:
" Hast thou perform'd my mission which I gave?
What is it thou hast seen? or what hast heard?"
  And answer made the bold Sir Bedivere:
" I heard the ripple washing in the reeds,   70
And the wild water lapping on the crag."
  To whom replied King Arthur, faint and pale:
" Thou hast betray'd thy nature and thy name,
Not rendering true answer, as beseem'd
Thy fealty, nor like a noble knight:
For surer sign had follow'd, either hand,
Or voice, or else a motion of the mere.
This is a shameful thing for men to lie.
Yet now, I charge thee, quickly go again
As thou art lief and dear, and do the thing   80
I bade thee, watch, and lightly bring me word."
  Then went Sir Bedivere the second time
Across the ridge, and paced beside the mere,
Counting the dewy pebbles, fix'd in thought;
But when he saw the wonder of the hilt,
How curiously and strangely chased, he smote
His palms together, and he cried aloud,
  " And if indeed I cast the brand away,
Surely a precious thing, one worthy note,
Should thus be lost for ever from the earth,   90
Which might have pleased the eyes of many men.
What good should follow this, if this were done?
What harm, undone? deep harm to disobey,
Seeing obedience is the bond of rule.
Were it well to obey then, if a king demand
An act unprofitable, against himself?
The King is sick, and knows not what he does.

What record, or what relic of my lord
Should be to aftertime, but empty breath
And rumours of a doubt ? but were this kept,   100
Stored in some treasure-house of mighty kings,
Some one might show it at a joust of arms,
Saying, ' King Arthur's sword, Excalibur,
Wrought by the lonely maiden of the Lake.
Nine years she wrought it, sitting in the deeps
Upon the hidden bases of the hills.'
So might some old man speak in the aftertime
To all the people, winning reverence.
But now much honour and much fame were lost."

    So spake he, clouded with his own conceit,   110
And hid Excalibur the second time,
And so strode back slow to the wounded King.

    Then spoke King Arthur, breathing heavily :
" What is it thou hast seen ? or what hast heard ? "

    And answer made the bold Sir Bedivere :
" I heard the water lapping on the crag,
And the long ripple washing in the reeds."

    To whom replied King Arthur, much in wrath :
"Ah, miserable and unkind, untrue,
Unknightly, traitor-hearted ! Woe is me !   120
Authority forgets a dying king,
Laid widow'd of the power in his eye
That bow'd the will.   I see thee what thou art,
For thou, the latest-left of all my knights,
In whom should meet the offices of all.
Thou wouldst betray me for the precious hilt ;
Either from lust of gold, or like a girl
Valuing the giddy pleasure of the eyes.
Yet, for a man may fail in duty twice,
And the third time may prosper, get thee hence :   130
But, if thou spare to fling Excalibur,
I will arise and slay thee with my hands."

Then quickly rose Sir Bedivere, and ran,
And, leaping down the ridges lightly, plunged
Among the bulrush-beds, and clutch'd the sword,
And strongly wheel'd and threw it. The great brand
Made lightnings in the splendour of the moon,
And flashing round and round, and whirl'd in an arch,
Shot like a streamer of the northern morn,
Seen where the moving isles of winter shock   140
By night, with noises of the northern sea.
So flash'd and fell the brand Excalibur:
But ere he dipt the surface, rose an arm
Clothed in white samite, mystic, wonderful,
And caught him by the hilt, and brandish'd him
Three times, and drew him under in the mere.
And lightly went the other to the King.

    Then spoke King Arthur, drawing thicker breath:
" Now see I by thine eyes that this is done.
Speak out: what is it thou hast heard or seen? "   150

    And answer made the bold Sir Bedivere:
" Sir King, I closed mine eyelids, lest the gems
Should blind my purpose, for I never saw,
Nor shall see, here or elsewhere, till I die,
Not tho' I live three lives of mortal men,
So great a miracle as yonder hilt.
Then with both hands I flung him, wheeling him;
But when I look'd again, behold an arm,
Clothed in white samite, mystic, wonderful,
That caught him by the hilt, and brandish'd him   160
Three times, and drew him under in the mere."

    And answer made King Arthur, breathing hard:
" My end draws nigh; 'tis time that I were gone.
Make broad thy shoulders to receive my weight,
And bear me to the margin; yet I fear
My wound hath taken cold, and I shall die."

    So saying, from the pavement he half rose,

Slowly, with pain, reclining on his arm,
And looking wistfully with wide blue eyes
As in a picture. Him Sir Bedivere   170
Remorsefully regarded thro' his tears,
And would have spoken, but he found not words,
Then took with care, and kneeling on one knee,
O'er both his shoulders drew the languid hands,
And rising bore him thro' the place of tombs.

    But, as he walk'd, King Arthur panted hard,
Like one that feels a nightmare on his bed
When all the house is mute. So sigh'd the King,
Muttering and murmuring at his ear, " Quick, quick !
I fear it is too late, and I shall die."   180
But the other swiftly strode from ridge to ridge,
Clothed with his breath, and looking, as he walk'd,
Larger than human on the frozen hills.
He heard the deep behind him, and a cry
Before. His own thought drove him, like a goad.
Dry clash'd his harness in the icy caves
And barren chasms, and all to left and right
The bare black cliff clang'd round him, as he based
His feet on juts of slippery crag that rang
Sharp-smitten with the dint of armed heels—   190
And on a sudden, lo ! the level lake,
And the long glories of the winter moon.

    Then saw they how there hove a dusky barge,
Dark as a funeral scarf from stem to stern,
Beneath them ; and descending they were ware
That all the decks were dense with stately forms
Black-stoled, black-hooded, like a dream—by these
Three Queens with crowns of gold—-and from them
        rose
A cry that shiver'd to the tingling stars,
And, as it were one voice an agony   200
Of lamentation, like a wind, that shrills

All night in a waste land, where no one comes,
Or hath come, since the making of the world.

  Then murmur'd Arthur, "Place me in the barge,"
And to the barge they came. There those three Queens
Put forth their hands, and took the King, and wept
But she, that rose the tallest of them all
And fairest, laid his head upon her lap,
And loosed the shatter'd casque, and chafed his hands,
And call'd him by his name, complaining loud,   210
And dropping bitter tears against his brow
Striped with dark blood : for all his face was white
And colourless, and like the wither'd moon
Smote by the fresh beam of the springing east ;
And all his greaves and cuisses dash'd with drops
Of onset ; and the light and lustrous curls—
That made his forehead like a rising sun
High from the daïs-throne—were parch'd with dust ;
Or, clotted into points and hanging loose,
Mix'd with the knightly growth that fringed his lips.
So like a shatter'd column lay the King ;   221
Not like that Arthur who, with lance in rest,
From spur to plume a star of tournament,
Shot thro' the lists at Camelot, and charged
Before the eyes of ladies and of kings.

  Then loudly cried the bold Sir Bedivere,
"Ah ! my Lord Arthur, whither shall I go ?
Where shall I hide my forehead and my eyes ?
For now I see the true old times are dead,
When every morning brought a noble chance,   230
And every chance brought out a noble knight.
Such times have been not since the light that led
The holy Elders with the gift of myrrh.
But now the whole ROUND TABLE is dissolved
Which was an image of the mighty world ;
And I, the last, go forth companionless,

And the days darken round me, and the years,
Among new men, strange faces, other minds."
  And slowly answered Arthur from the barge:
" The old order changeth, yielding place to new, 240
And God fulfils Himself in many ways,
Lest one good custom should corrupt the world.
Comfort thyself: what comfort is in me?
I have lived my life, and that which I have done
May He within Himself make pure! but thou,
If thou shouldst never see my face again,
Pray for my soul. More things are wrought by prayer
Than this world dreams of. Wherefore, let thy voice
Rise like a fountain for me night and day.
For what are men better than sheep or goats 250
That nourish a blind life within the brain,
If, knowing God, they lift not hands of prayer
Both for themselves and those who call them friend?
For so the whole round earth is every way
Bound by gold chains about the feet of God.
But now farewell. I am going a long way
With these thou seest—if indeed I go—
(For all my mind is clouded with a doubt)
To the island-valley of Avilion;
Where falls not hail, or rain, or any snow, 260
Nor ever wind blows loudly; but it lies
Deep-meadow'd, happy, fair with orchard lawns
And bowery hollows crown'd with summer sea,
Where I will heal me of my grievous wound."
  So said he, and the barge with oar and sail
Moved from the brink, like some full-breasted swan
That, fluting a wild carol ere her death,
Ruffles her pure cold plume, and takes the flood
With swarthy webs. Long stood Sir Bedivere

Revolving many memories, till the hull   270
Look'd one black dot against the verge of dawn,
And on the mere the wailing died away.

II.—ARNOLD

SOHRAB AND RUSTUM

And the first grey of morning fill'd the east,
And the fog rose out of the Oxus stream.
But all the Tartar camp along the stream
Was hush'd, and still the men were plunged in sleep :
Sohrab alone, he slept not : all night long
He had lain wakeful, tossing on his bed ;
But when the grey dawn stole into his tent,
He rose, and clad himself, and girt his sword,
And took his horseman's cloak, and left his tent,
And went abroad into the cold wet fog,   10
Through the dim camp to Peran-Wisa's tent.

    Through the black Tartar tents he pass'd, which stood
Clustering like bee-hives on the low flat strand
Of Oxus, where the summer floods o'erflow
When the sun melts the snows in high Pamere :
Through the black tents he pass'd, o'er that low strand,
And to a hillock came, a little back
From the stream's brink, the spot where first a boat,
Crossing the stream in summer, scrapes the land.
The men of former times had crown'd the top   20
With a clay fort : but that was fall'n ; and now
The Tartars built there Peran-Wisa's tent,
A dome of laths, and o'er it felts were spread.
And Sohrab came there, and went in, and stood
Upon the thick-piled carpets in the tent,
And found the old man sleeping on his bed
Of rugs and felts, and near him lay his arms.

And Peran-Wisa heard him, though the step
Was dull'd ; for he slept light, an old man's sleep ;
And he rose quickly on one arm, and said :—   30
    " Who art thou ? for it is not yet clear dawn.
Speak ! is there news, or any night alarm ? "
    But Sohrab came to the bedside, and said :—
" Thou know'st me, Peran-Wisa : it is I.
The sun is not yet risen, and the foe
Sleep ; but I sleep not ; all night long I lie
Tossing and wakeful, and I come to thee.
For so did King Afrasiab bid me seek
Thy counsel, and to heed thee as thy son,
In Samarcand, before the army march'd ;   40
And I will tell thee what my heart desires.
Thou knowest if, since from Ader-baijan first
I came among the Tartars, and bore arms,
I have still served Afrasiab well, and shown,
At my boy's years, the courage of a man.
This too thou know'st, that, while I still bear on
The conquering Tartar ensigns through the world,
And beat the Persians back on every field,
I seek one man, one man, and one alone—
Rustum, my father ; who, I hoped, should greet,   50
Should one day greet, upon some well-fought field,
His not unworthy, not inglorious son.
So I long hoped, but him I never find.
Come then, hear now, and grant me what I ask.
Let the two armies rest to-day : but I
Will challenge forth the bravest Persian lords
To meet me, man to man : if I prevail,
Rustum will surely hear it ; if I fall—
Old man, the dead need no one, claim no kin.
Dim is the rumour of a common fight,   60
Where host meets host, and many names are sunk :
But of a single combat fame speaks clear."

He spoke : and Peran-Wisa took the hand
Of the young man in his, and sigh'd, and said :—
    " O Sohrab, an unquiet heart is thine !
Canst thou not rest among the Tartar chiefs,
And share the battle's common chance with us
Who love thee, but must press for ever first,
In single fight incurring single risk,
To find a father thou hast never seen ?   70
That were far best, my son, to stay with us
Unmurmuring ; in our tents, while it is war,
And when 'tis truce, then in Afrasiab's towns.
But, if this one desire indeed rules all,
To seek out Rustum—seek him not through fight :
Seek him in peace, and carry to his arms,
O Sohrab, carry an unwounded son !
But far hence seek him, for he is not here.
For now it is not as when I was young,
When Rustum was in front of every fray :   80
But now he keeps apart, and sits at home,
In Seistan, with Zal, his father old.
Whether that his own mighty strength at last
Feels the abhorr'd approaches of old age ;
Or in some quarrel with the Persian King.
There go !—Thou wilt not ? Yet my heart forebodes
Danger or death awaits thee on this field.
Fain would I know thee safe and well, though lost
To us : fain therefore send thee hence, in peace
To seek thy father, not seek single fights   90
In vain :—but who can keep the lion's cub
From ravening ? and who govern Rustum's son ?
Go : I will grant thee what thy heart desires."
    So said he, and dropp'd Sohrab's hand, and left
His bed, and the warm rugs whereon he lay,
And o'er his chilly limbs his woollen coat
He pass'd, and tied his sandals on his feet.

And threw a white cloak round him, and he took
In his right hand a ruler's staff, no sword ;
    And on his head he set his sheep-skin cap,   100
Black, glossy, curl'd, the fleece of Kara-Kul ;
And raised the curtain of his tent, and call'd
His herald to his side, and went abroad.

    The sun, by this, had risen, and clear'd the fog
From the broad Oxus and the glittering sands :
And from their tents the Tartar horsemen filed
Into the open plain ; so Haman bade ;
Haman, who next to Peran-Wisa ruled
The host, and still was in his lusty prime.
From their black tents, long files of horse, they stream'd
As when, some grey November morn, the files,   111
In marching order spread, of long-neck'd cranes
Stream over Casbin, and the southern slopes
Of Elburz, from the Aralian estuaries,
Or some frore Caspian reed-bed, southward bound —
For the warm Persian sea-board : so they stream'd.
The Tartars of the Oxus, the King's guard,
First, with black sheep-skin caps and with long spears ;
Large men, large steeds ; who from Bokhara come
And Khiva, and ferment the milk of mares.   120
Next the more temperate Toorkmuns of the south,
The Tukas, and the lances of Salore,
And those from Attruck and the Caspian sands ;
Light men, and on light steeds, who only drink
The acrid milk of camels, and their wells.
And then a swarm of wandering horse, who came
From afar, and a more doubtful service own'd ;
The Tartars of Ferghana, from the banks
Of the Jaxartes, men with scanty beards
And close-set skull-caps ; and those wilder hordes   130
Who roam o'er Kipchak and the northern waste,
Kalmuks and unkemp'd Kuzzaks, tribes who stray

Nearest the Pole, and wandering Kirghizzes,
Who come on shaggy ponies from Pamere.
These all filed out from camp into the plain.
And on the other side the Persians form'd :
First a light cloud of horse, Tartars they seem'd,
The Ilyats of Khorassan : and behind,
The royal troops of Persia, horse and foot,
Marshall'd battalions bright in burnish'd steel.   140
But Peran-Wisa with his herald came
Threading the Tartar squadrons to the front,
And with his staff kept back the foremost ranks.
And when Ferood, who led the Persians, saw
That Peran-Wisa kept the Tartars back,
He took his spear, and to the front he came,
And check'd his ranks, and fix'd them where they stood.
And the old Tartar came upon the sand
Betwixt the silent hosts, and spake, and said :—

    " Ferood, and ye, Persians and Tartars, hear !   150
Let there be truce between the hosts to-day.
But choose a champion from the Persian lords
To fight our champion Sohrab, man to man."

    As, in the country, on a morn in June,
When the dew glistens on the pearled ears,
A shiver runs through the deep corn for joy—
So, when they heard what Peran-Wisa said,
A thrill through all the Tartar squadrons ran
Of pride and hope for Sohrab, whom they loved.

    But as a troop of pedlars, from Cabool,   160
Cross underneath the Indian Caucasus,
That vast sky-neighbouring mountain of milk snow ;
Crossing so high, that, as they mount, they pass
Long flocks of travelling birds dead on the snow,
Choked by the air, and scarce can they themselves
Slake their parch'd throats with sugar'd mulberries—
In single file they move, and stop their breath,

For fear they should dislodge the o'erhanging snows—
So the pale Persians held their breath with fear.

    And to Ferood his brother chiefs came up   170
To counsel: Gudurz and Zoarrah came,
And Feraburz, who ruled the Persian host
Second, and was the uncle of the King:
These came and counsell'd; and then Gudurz said:—
" Ferood, shame bids us take their challenge up,
Yet champion have we none to match this youth.
He has the wild stag's foot, the lion's heart.
But Rustum came last night; aloof he sits
And sullen, and has pitch'd his tents apart:
Him will I seek, and carry to his ear   180
The Tartar challenge, and this young man's name.
Haply he will forget his wrath, and fight.
Stand forth the while, and take their challenge up."
So spake he; and Ferood stood forth and cried:—
" Old man, be it agreed as thou hast said.
Let Sohrab arm, and we will find a man."

    He spoke; and Peran-Wisa turn'd, and strode
Back through the opening squadrons to his tent.
But through the anxious Persians Gudurz ran,
And cross'd the camp which lay behind, and reach'd,   190
Out on the sands beyond it, Rustum's tents.
Of scarlet cloth they were, and glittering gay,
Just pitch'd: the high pavilion in the midst
Was Rustum's, and his men lay camp'd around.
And Gudurz enter'd Rustum's tent, and found
Rustum: his morning meal was done, but still
The table stood beside him, charged with food;
A side of roasted sheep, and cakes of bread,
And dark green melons; and there Rustum sate
Listless, and held a falcon on his wrist,   200
And play'd with it; but Gudurz came and stood
Before him; and he look'd, and saw him stand;

And with a cry sprang up, and dropp'd the bird,
And greeted Gudurz with both hands, and said :—
    " Welcome ! these eyes could see no better sight.
What news ? but sit down first, and eat and drink."
    But Gudurz stood in the tent door, and said :—
" Not now : a time will come to eat and drink,
But not to-day : to-day has other needs.
The armies are drawn out, and stand at gaze :   210
For from the Tartars is a challenge brought
To pick a champion from the Persian lords
To fight their champion—and thou know'st his name—
Sohrab men call him, but his birth is hid.
O Rustum, like thy might is this young man's !
He has the wild stag's foot, the lion's heart.
And he is young and Iran's chiefs are old,
Or else too weak ; and all eyes turn to thee.
Come down and help us, Rustum, or we lose."
    He spoke : but Rustum answer'd with a smile :— 220
" Go to ! if Iran's chiefs are old, then I
Am older : if the young are weak, the King
Errs strangely : for the King, for Kai Khosroo,
Himself is young, and honours younger men,
And lets the aged moulder to their graves.
Rustum he loves no more, but loves the young—
The young may rise at Sohrab's vaunts, not I.
For what care I, though all speak Sohrab's fame ?
For would that I myself had such a son,
And not that one slight helpless girl I have—   230
A son so famed, so brave, to send to war,
And I to tarry with the snow-hair'd Zal,
My father, whom the robber Afghans vex,
And clip his borders short, and drive his herds,
And he has none to guard his weak old age.
There would I go, and hang my armour up,
And with my great name fence that weak old man,

And spend the goodly treasures I have got,
And rest my age, and hear of Sohrab's fame,
And leave to death the hosts of thankless kings,   240
And with these slaughterous hands draw sword no more."

He spoke, and smiled ; and Gudurz made reply :—
" What then, O Rustum, will men say to this,
When Sohrab dares our bravest forth, and seeks
Thee most of all, and thou, whom most he seeks,
Hidest thy face ? Take heed, lest men should say,
Like some old miser, Rustum hoards his fame,
And shuns to peril it with younger men."

And, greatly moved, then Rustum made reply :—
" O Gudurz, wherefore dost thou say such words ?   250
Thou knowest better words than this to say.
What is one more, one less, obscure or famed,
Valiant or craven, young or old, to me ?
Are not they mortal, am not I myself ?
But who for men of nought would do great deeds ?
Come, thou shalt see how Rustum hoards his fame.
But I will fight unknown, and in plain arms ;
Let not men say of Rustum, he was match'd
In single fight with any mortal man."

He spoke, and frown'd; and Gudurz turn'd, and ran 260
Back quickly through the camp in fear and joy,
Fear at his wrath, but joy that Rustum came.
But Rustum strode to his tent door, and call'd
His followers in, and bade them bring his arms,
And clad himself in steel : the arms he chose
Were plain, and on his shield was no device,
Only his helm was rich, inlaid with gold,
And from the fluted spine atop a plume
Of horsehair waved, a scarlet horsehair plume.
So arm'd he issued forth ; and Ruksh, his horse,   270
Follow'd him, like a faithful hound, at heel—
Ruksh, whose renown was noised through all the earth

The horse, whom Rustum on a foray once
Did in Bokhara by the river find
A colt beneath its dam, and drove him home,
And rear'd him ; a bright bay, with lofty crest,
Dight with a saddle-cloth of broider'd green
Crusted with gold, and on the ground were work'd
All beasts of chase, all beasts which hunters know.
So follow'd, Rustum left his tents, and cross'd   280
The camp, and to the Persian host appear'd.
And all the Persians knew him, and with shouts
Hail'd ; but the Tartars knew not who he was.
And dear as the wet diver to the eyes
Of his pale wife who waits and weeps on shore,
By sandy Bahrein, in the Persian Gulf,
Plunging all day in the blue waves, at night,
Having made up his tale of precious pearls,
Rejoins her in their hut upon the sands—
So dear to the pale Persians Rustum came.   290

    And Rustum to the Persian front advanced,
And Sohrab arm'd in Haman's tent, and came.
And as afield the reapers cut a swathe
Down through the middle of a rich man's corn,
And on each side are squares of standing corn,
And in the midst a stubble, short and bare—
So on each side were squares of men, with spears
Bristling, and in the midst, the open sand.
And Rustum came upon the sand, and cast
His eyes toward the Tartar tents, and saw   300
Sohrab come forth, and eyed him as he came.

    As some rich woman, on a winter's morn,
Eyes through her silken curtains the poor drudge
Who with numb blacken'd fingers makes her fire—
At cock-crow, on a starlit winter's morn,
When the frost flowers the whiten'd window panes—
And wonders how she lives, and what the thoughts

Of that poor drudge may be—so Rustum eyed
The unknown adventurous youth, who from afar
Came seeking Rustum, and defying forth   310
All the most valiant chiefs : long he perused
His spirited air, and wonder'd who he was.
For very young he seem'd, tenderly rear'd ;
Like some young cypress, tall, and dark, and straight,
Which in a queen's secluded garden throws
Its slight dark shadow on the moonlit turf,
By midnight, to a bubbling fountain's sound—
So slender Sohrab seem'd, so softly rear'd.
And a deep pity enter'd Rustum's soul
As he beheld him coming ; and he stood,   320
And beckon'd to him with his hand, and said :—

   " O thou young man, the air of Heaven is soft,
And warm, and pleasant ; but the grave is cold.
Heaven's air is better than the cold dead grave.
Behold me ! I am vast, and clad in iron,
And tried ; and I have stood on many a field
Of blood, and I have fought with many a foe :
Never was that field lost, or that foe saved.
O Sohrab, wherefore wilt thou rush on death ?
Be govern'd ! quit the Tartar host, and come   330
To Iran, and be as my son to me,
And fight beneath my banner till I die !
There are no youths in Iran brave as thou."

   So he spake, mildly : Sohrab heard his voice,
The mighty voice of Rustum ; and he saw
His giant figure planted on the sand,
Sole, like some single tower, which a chief
Has builded on the waste in former years
Against the robbers ; and he saw that head,
Streak'd with its first grey hairs ;—hope fill'd his soul ;
And he ran forwards and embraced his knees,   341
And clasp'd his hand within his own and said :—

" Oh, by thy father's head ! by thine own soul !
Art thou not Rustum ? Speak ! art thou not he ? "

But Rustum eyed askance the kneeling youth,
And turned away, and spake to his own soul :—

"Ah me, I muse what this young fox may mean.
False, wily, boastful, are these Tartar boys.
For if I now confess this thing he asks,
And hide it not, but say—*Rustum is here*—   350
He will not yield indeed, nor quit our foes,
But he will find some pretext not to fight,
And praise my fame, and proffer courteous gifts.
A belt or sword perhaps, and go his way.
And on a feast-tide, in Afrasiab's hall,
In Samarcand, he will arise and cry :—
' I challenged once, when the two armies camp'd
Beside the Oxus, all the Persian lords
To cope with me in single fight ; but they
Shrank ; only Rustum dar'd : then he and I   360
Changed gifts, and went on equal terms away.'
So will he speak, perhaps, while men applaud.
Then were the chiefs of Iran shamed through me."

And then he turn'd, and sternly spake aloud :—
" Rise ! wherefore dost thou vainly question thus
Of Rustum ? I am here, whom thou hast call'd
By challenge forth : make good thy vaunt, or yield !
Is it with Rustum only thou would'st fight ?
Rash boy, men look on Rustum's face and flee !
For well I know, that did great Rustum stand   370
Before thy face this day, and were reveal'd,
There would be then no talk of fighting more.
But being what I am, I tell thee this ;
Do thou record it in thy inmost soul :
Either thou shalt renounce thy vaunt, and yield ;
Or else thy bones shall strew this sand, till winds
Bleach them, or Oxus with his summer floods,
Oxus in summer wash them all away."

He spoke : and Sohrab answer'd, on his feet :—
"Art thou so fierce ? Thou wilt not fright me so ! 380
I am no girl, to be made pale by words.
Yet this thou hast said well, did Rustum stand
Here on this field, there were no fighting then.
But Rustum is far hence, and we stand here.
Begin ! thou art more vast, more dread than I,
And thou art proved, I know, and I am young—
But yet success sways with the breath of Heaven.
And though thou thinkest that thou knowest sure
Thy victory, yet thou canst not surely know.
For we are all, like swimmers in the sea, 390
Poised on the top of a huge wave of Fate,
Which hangs uncertain to which side to fall.
And whether it will heave us up to land,
Or whether it will roll us out to sea,
Back out to sea, to the deep waves of death,
We know not, and no search will make us know :
Only the event will teach us in its hour."

He spoke ; and Rustum answer'd not, but hurl'd
His spear : down from the shoulder, down it came,
As on some partridge in the corn a hawk, 400
That long has tower'd in the airy clouds,
Drops like a plummet : Sohrab saw it come,
And sprang aside, quick as a flash : the spear
Hiss'd, and went quivering down into the sand,
Which it sent flying wide ;—then Sorab threw
In turn, and full struck Rustum's shield : sharp rang,
The iron plates rang sharp, but turn'd the spear.
And Rustum seized his club, which none but he
Could wield : an unlopp'd trunk it was, and huge,
Still rough ; like those which men in treeless plains 410
To build them boats fish from the flooded rivers,
Hyphasis or Hydaspes, when, high up
By their dark springs, the wind in winter-time
Hath made in Himalayan forests wrack,

B

And strewn the channels with torn boughs—so huge
The club which Rustum lifted now, and struck
One stroke ; but again Sohrab sprang aside,
Lithe as the glancing snake, and the club came
Thundering to earth, and leapt from Rustum's hand.
And Rustum follow'd his own blow, and fell   420
To his knees, and with his fingers clutch'd the sand :
And now might Sohrab have unsheathed his sword,
And pierced the mighty Rustum while he lay
Dizzy, and on his knees, and choked with sand :
But he look'd on, and smiled, nor bared his sword,
But courteously drew back, and spoke, and said :—
    " Thou strik'st too hard : that club of thine will
        float
Upon the summer floods and not my bones,
But rise, and be not wroth ; not wroth am I :
No, when I see thee, wrath forsakes my soul.   430
Thou say'st, thou art not Rustum : be it so.
Who art thou then, that canst so touch my soul ?
Boy as I am, I have seen battles too—
Have waded foremost in their bloody waves,
And heard their hollow roar of dying men ;
But never was my heart thus touch'd before.
Are they from Heaven, these softenings of the heart ?
O thou old warrior, let us yield to Heaven !
Come, plant we here in earth, our angry spears,
And make a truce, and sit upon this sand,   440
And pledge each other in red wine, like friends,
And thou shalt talk to me of Rustum's deeds.
There are enough foes in the Persian host
Whom I may meet, and strike, and feel no pang ;
Champions enough Afrasiab has, whom thou
Mayst fight ; fight them, when they confront thy
        spear.
But oh, let there be peace 'twixt thee and me ! "

He ceased : but while he spake, Rustum had risen,
And stood erect, trembling with rage : his club
He left to lie, but had regain'd his spear,   450
Whose fiery point now in his mail'd right-hand
Blazed bright and baleful, like that autumn star,
The baleful sign of fevers : dust had soil'd
His stately crest, and dimm'd his glittering arms.
His breast heaved ; his lips foam'd ; and twice his voice
Was choked with rage : at last these words broke way :—
    " Girl ! nimble with thy feet, not with thy hands !
Curl'd minion, dancer, coiner of sweet words !
Fight ; let me hear thy hateful voice no more !
Thou art not in Afrasiab's gardens now   460
With Tartar girls, with whom thou art wont to dance ;
But on the Oxus sands, and in the dance
Of battle, and with me, who make no play
Of war : I fight it out, and hand to hand.
Speak not to me of truce, and pledge, and wine !
Remember all thy valour : try thy feints
And cunning : all the pity I had is gone :
Because thou hast shamed me before both the hosts
With thy light skipping tricks, and thy girls' wiles."
    He spoke ; and Sohrab kindled at his taunts,   470
And he too drew his sword : at once they rush'd
Together, as two eagles on one prey
Come rushing down together from the clouds,
One from the east, one from the west : their shields
Dash'd with a clang together, and a din
Rose, such as that the sinewy woodcutters
Make often in the forest's heart at morn,
Of hewing axes, crashing trees—such blows
Rustum and Sohrab on each other hail'd.
And you would say that sun and stars took part   480
In that unnatural conflict ; for a cloud
Grew suddenly in Heaven, and dark'd the sun

Over the fighters' heads ; and a wind rose
Under their feet, and moaning swept the plain,
And in a sandy whirlwind wrapp'd the pair.
In gloom they twain were wrapp'd, and they alone ;
For both the on-looking hosts on either hand
Stood in broad daylight, and the sky was pure,
And the sun sparkled on the Oxus stream.
But in the gloom they fought, with bloodshot eyes   490
And labouring breath ; first Rustum struck the shield
Which Sohrab held stiff out : the steel-spiked spear
Rent the tough plates, but fail'd to reach the skin,
And Rustum pluck'd it back with angry groan.
Then Sohrab with his sword smote Rustum's helm,
Nor clove its steel quite through ; but all the crest
He shore away, and that proud horsehair plume,
Never till now defiled, sank to the dust ;
And Rustum bow'd his head ; but then the gloom
Grew blacker : thunder rumbled in the air,   500
And lightnings rent the cloud ; and Ruksh, the horse,
Who stood at hand, utter'd a dreadful cry :
No horse's cry was that, most like the roar
Of some pain'd desert lion, who all day
Has trail'd the hunter's javelin in his side,
And comes at night to die upon the sand ;—
The two hosts heard that cry, and quaked for fear,
And Oxus curdled as it cross'd his stream.
But Sohrab heard, and quail'd not, but rush'd on,
And struck again ; and again Rustum bow'd   510
His head ; but this time all the blade, like glass,
Sprang in a thousand shivers on the helm,
And in the hand the hilt remain'd alone.
Then Rustum raised his head : his dreadful eyes
Glared, and he shook on high his menacing spear,
And shouted, *Rustum !*—Sohrab heard that shout,
And shrank amazed : back he recoil'd one step,

And scann'd with blinking eyes the advancing form :
And then he stood bewilder'd ; and he dropp'd
His covering shield, and the spear pierced his side.   520
He reel'd, and staggering back, sunk to the ground.
And then the gloom dispersed, and the wind fell,
And the bright sun broke forth, and melted all
The cloud ; and the two armies saw the pair :—
Saw Rustum standing, safe upon his feet,
And Sohrab, wounded, on the bloody sand.

   Then, with a bitter smile, Rustum began :—
" Sohrab, thou thoughtest in thy mind to kill
A Persian lord this day, and strip his corpse,
And bear thy trophies to Afrasiab's tent.   530
Or else that the great Rustum would come down
Himself to fight, and that thy wiles would move
His heart to take a gift, and let thee go.
And then that all the Tartar host would praise
Thy courage or thy craft, and spread thy fame,
To glad thy father in his weak old age.
Fool ! thou art slain, and by an unknown man !
Dearer to the red jackals shalt thou be,
Than to thy friends, and to thy father old."

   And with a fearless mien Sohrab replied :—   540
" Unknown thou art ; yet thy fierce vaunt is vain.
Thou dost not slay me, proud and boastful man !
No ! Rustum slays me, and this filial heart.
For were I match'd with ten such men as thee,
And I were that which till to-day I was,
They should be lying here, I standing there.
But that belovèd name unnerved my arm—
That name, and something, I confess, in thee,
Which troubles all my heart, and made my shield
Fall ; and thy spear transfix'd an unarm'd foe.   550
And now thou boastest and insult'st my fate.
But hear thou this, fierce man, tremble to hear :

The mighty Rustum shall avenge my death !
My father, whom I seek through all the world,
He shall avenge my death, and punish thee ! "
    As when some hunter in the spring hath found
A breeding eagle sitting on her nest,
Upon the craggy isle of a hill lake,
And pierced her with an arrow as she rose,
And follow'd her to find out where she fell   560
Far off ;—anon her mate comes winging back
From hunting, and a great way off descries
His huddling young left sole ; at that, he checks
His pinion, and with short uneasy sweeps
Circles above his eyry, with loud screams
Chiding his mate back to her nest ; but she
Lies dying, with the arrow in her side,
In some far stony gorge out of his ken,
A heap of fluttering feathers : never more
Shall the lake glass her, flying over it ;   570
Never the black and dripping precipices
Echo her stormy scream as she sails by ;—
As that poor bird flies home, nor knows his loss,
So Rustum knew not his own loss, but stood
Over his dying son, and knew him not.
    But with a cold, incredulous voice, he said :—
" What prate is this of fathers and revenge ?
The mighty Rustum never had a son."
    And, with a failing voice, Sohrab replied :—
"Ah yes, he had ! and that lost son am I.   580
Surely the news will one day reach his ear,
Reach Rustum, where he sits, and tarries long,
Somewhere, I know not where, but far from here ;
And pierce him like a stab, and make him leap
To arms, and cry for vengeance upon thee.
Fierce man, bethink thee, for an only son !
What will that grief, what will that vengeance be ?

Oh, could I live, till I that grief had seen !
Yet him I pity not so much, but her,
My mother, who in Ader-baijan dwells   590
With that old king, her father, who grows grey
With age, and rules over the valiant Koords.
Her most I pity, who no more will see
Sohrab returning from the Tartar camp,
With spoils and honour, when the war is done.
But a dark rumour will be bruited up,
From tribe to tribe, until it reach her ear ;
And then will that defenceless woman learn
That Sohrab will rejoice her sight no more ;
But that in battle with a nameless foe,   600
By the far-distant Oxus, he is slain."
   He spoke ; and as he ceased he wept aloud,
Thinking of her he left, and his own death.
He spoke ; but Rustum listen'd, plunged in thought.
Nor did he yet believe it was his son
Who spoke, although he call'd back names he knew ;
For he had had sure tidings that the babe,
Which was in Ader-baijan born to him,
Had been a puny girl, no boy at all—
So that sad mother sent him word, for fear   610
Rustum should take the boy, to train in arms.
And so he deem'd that either Sohrab took,
By a false boast, the style of Rustum's son ;
Or that men gave it him, to swell his fame.
So deem'd he ; yet he listen'd, plunged in thought ;
And his soul set to grief, as the vast tide
Of the bright rocking Ocean sets to shore
At the full moon : tears gathered in his eyes ;
For he remember'd his own early youth,
And all its bounding rapture ; as, at dawn,   620
The shepherd from his mountain lodge descries
A far bright city, smitten by the sun,

Through many rolling clouds ;—so Rustum saw
His youth ; saw Sohrab's mother, in her bloom ;
And that old king, her father, who loved well
His wandering guest, and gave him his fair child
With joy ; and all the pleasant life they led,
They three, in that long distant summer-time—
The castle, and the dewy woods, and hunt
And hound, and morn on those delightful hills   630
In Ader-baijan. And he saw that Youth,
Of age and looks to be his own dear son,
Piteous and lovely, lying on the sand,
Like some rich hyacinth, which by the scythe
Of an unskilful gardener has been cut,
Mowing the garden grass-plots near its bed,
And lies, a fragrant tower of purple bloom,
On the mown, dying grass ;—so Sohrab lay,
Lovely in death, upon the common sand.
And Rustum gazed on him with grief, and said :—   640
    " O Sohrab, thou indeed art such a son
Whom Rustum, wert thou his, might well have loved !
Yet here thou errest, Sohrab, or else men
Have told thee false ;—thou art not Rustum's son.
For Rustum had no son : one child he had—
But one—a girl : who with her mother now
Plies some light female task, nor dreams of us—
Of us she dreams not, nor of wounds, nor war."
But Sohrab answer'd him in wrath ; for now
The anguish of the deep-fix'd spear grew fierce,   650
And he desired to draw forth the steel,
And let the blood flow free, and so to die ;
But first he would convince his stubborn foe—
And, rising sternly on one arm, he said :—
" Man, who art thou who dost deny my words ?
Truth sits upon the lips of dying men,
And falsehood, while I lived, was far from mine.

I tell thee, prick'd upon this arm I bear
That seal which Rustum to my mother gave,
That she might prick it on the babe she bore."   660
   He spoke : and all the blood left Rustum's cheeks ;
And his knees totter'd, and he smote his hand
Against his breast, his heavy mailed hand,
That the hard iron corslet clank'd aloud :
And to his heart he press'd the other hand,
And in a hollow voice he spake, and said :—
   " Sohrab, that were a proof which could not lie.
If thou show this, then art thou Rustum's son."
   Then, with weak hasty fingers, Sohrab loosed
His belt, and near the shoulder bared his arm,   670
And show'd a sign in faint vermilion points
Prick'd : as a cunning workman, in Pekin,
Pricks with vermilion some clear porcelain vase,
An emperor's gift—at early morn he paints,
And all day long, and, when night comes, the lamp
Lights up his studious forehead and thin hands ;—
So delicately prick'd the sign appear'd
On Sohrab's arm, the sign of Rustum's seal.
It was that griffin, which of old rear'd Zal,
Rustum's great father, whom they left to die,   680
A helpless babe, among the mountain rocks.
Him that kind creature found, and rear'd, and loved—
Then Rustum took it for his glorious sign.
And Sohrab bared that figure on his arm,
And himself scann'd it long with mournful eyes,
And then he touch'd it with his hand and said :—
   " How say'st thou ? Is that sign the proper sign
Of Rustum's son, or of some other man's ? "
   He spoke : but Rustum gazed, and gazed, and stood
Speechless ; and then he utter'd one sharp cry—   690
Oh boy—thy father !—and his voice choked there.
And then a dark cloud pass'd before his eyes,

B*

And his head swam, and he sank down to earth.
But Sohrab crawl'd to where he lay, and cast
His arms about his neck, and kiss'd his lips,
And with fond faltering fingers stroked his cheeks
Trying to call him back to life : and life
Came back to Rustum, and he oped his eyes
And they stood wide with horror ; and he seized
In both his hands the dust which lay around,   700
And threw it on his head, and smirch'd his hair—
His hair, and face, and beard, and glittering arms :
And strong convulsive groanings shook his breast,
And his sobs choked him ; and he clutch'd his sword,
To draw it, and for ever let life out.
But Sohrab saw his thought, and held his hands,
And with a soothing voice he spoke, and said :—
    " Father, forbear : for I but meet to-day
The doom that at my birth was written down
In Heaven, and thou art Heaven's unconscious hand. 710
Surely my heart cried out that it was thou,
When first I saw thee ; and thy heart spoke too,
I know it : but Fate trod those promptings down
Under its iron heel ; Fate, Fate engaged
The strife and hurl'd me on my father's spear.
But let us speak no more of this : I find
My father ; let me feel that I have found !
Come, sit beside me on this sand, and take
My head betwixt thy hands, and kiss my cheeks,
And wash them with thy tears, and say, *My son !*   720
Quick ! quick ! for number'd are my sands of life,
And swift ; for like the lightning to this field
I came, and like the wind I go away—
Sudden, and swift, and like a passing wind.
But it was writ in Heaven that this should be."
    So said he : and his voice released the heart
Of Rustum, and his tears broke forth ; he cast

His arms round his son's neck, and wept aloud,
And kiss'd him. And awe fell on both the hosts
When they saw Rustum's grief: and Ruksh, the horse, 730
With his head bowing to the ground, and mane
Sweeping the dust, came near, and in mute woe
First to the one then to the other moved
His head, as if enquiring what their grief
Might mean ; and from his dark, compassionate eyes,
The big warm tears roll'd down, and caked the sand.
But Rustum chid him with stern voice, and said :—

  "Ruksh, now thou grievest ; but, O Ruksh, thy feet
Should first have rotted on their nimble joints,
Or ere they brought thy master to this field."   740

  But Sohrab look'd upon the horse and said :—
"Is this then Ruksh ? How often, in past days,
My mother told me of thee, thou brave steed,
My terrible father's terrible horse ! and said,
That I should one day find thy lord and thee.

Come, let me lay my hand upon thy mane.
O Ruksh, thou art more fortunate than I ;
For thou hast gone where I shall never go,
And snuff'd the breezes of my father's home.
And thou hast trod the sands of Seistan,   750
And seen the river of Helmund, and the lake
Of Zirrah ; and the aged Zal himself
Has often stroked thy neck, and given thee food,
Corn in a golden platter soak'd with wine,
And said—' O Ruksh ! bear Rustum well ! '—but I
Have never known my grandsire's furrow'd face,
Nor seen his lofty house in Seistan,
Nor slaked my thirst at the clear Helmund stream :
But lodged among my father's foes, and seen
Afrasiab's cities only, Samarcand,   760
Bokhara, and lone Khiva in the waste,
And the black Toorkmun tents ; and only drunk

The desert rivers, Moorghab and Tejend,
Kohik, and where the Kalmuks feed their sheep,
The northern Sir ; and this great Oxus stream—
The yellow Oxus, by whose brink I die."

    And, with a heavy groan, Rustum bewail'd :—
" Oh, that its waves were flowing over me !
Oh, that I saw its grains of yellow silt
Roll tumbling in the current o'er my head ! "   770

    But, with a grave mild voice, Sohrab replied :—
" Desire not that, my father ; thou must live.
For some are born to do great deeds, and live,
As some are born to be obscured, and die.
Do thou the deeds I die too young to do,
And reap a second glory in thine age.
Thou art my father, and thy gain is mine.
But come ! thou seest this great host of men
Which follow me ; I pray thee, slay not these :
Let me entreat for them : what have they done ?   780
They follow'd me, my hope, my fame, my star.
Let them all cross the Oxus back in peace.
But me thou must bear hence, not send with them,
But carry me with thee to Seistan,
And place me on a bed, and mourn for me,
Thou, and the snow-hair'd Zal, and all thy friends.
And thou must lay me in that lovely earth,
And heap a stately mound above my bones,
And plant a far-seen pillar over all :
That so the passing horseman on the waste   790
May see my tomb a great way off, and cry :—
Sohrab, the mighty Rustum's son, lies there,
Whom his great father did in ignorance kill—
And I be not forgotten in my grave."

    And, with a mournful voice, Rustum replied :—
" Fear not ; as thou hast said, Sohrab, my son,
So shall it be : for I will burn my tents,

And quit the host, and bear thee hence with me,
And carry thee away to Seistan,
And place thee on a bed, and mourn for thee,   800
With the snow-headed Zal, and all my friends.
And I will lay thee in that lovely earth,
And heap a stately mount above thy bones,
And plant a far-seen pillar over all :
And men shall not forget thee in thy grave.
And I will spare thy host : yea, let them go :
Let them all cross the Oxus back in peace.
What should I do with slaying any more ?
For would that all whom I have ever slain
Might be once more alive—my bitterest foes,   810
And they who were call'd champions in their time,
And through whose death I won that fame I have—
And I were nothing but a common man,
A poor, mean soldier, and without renown ;
So thou mightest live too, my son, my son !
Or rather would that I, even I myself,
Might now be lying on this bloody sand,
Near death, and by an ignorant stroke of thine,
Not thou of mine ; and I might die, not thou ;
And I, not thou, be borne to Seistan ;   820
And Zal might weep above my grave, not thine ;
And say—*O son, I weep thee not too sore,*
For willingly, I know, thou met'st thine end !—
But now in blood and battles was my youth,
And full of blood and battles is my age ;
And I shall never end this life of blood."

    Then, at the point of death, Sohrab replied :—
"A life of blood indeed, thou dreadful man !
But thou shalt yet have peace ; only not now,
Not yet, but thou shalt have it on that day,   830
When thou shalt sail in a high-masted ship,
Thou and the other peers of Kai-Khosroo

Returning home over the salt blue sea,
From laying thy dear master in his grave."
    And Rustum gazed in Sohrab's face and said :—
" Soon be that day, my son, and deep that sea !
Till then, if fate so wills, let me endure."
    He spoke; and Sohrab smiled on him, and took
The spear, and drew it from his side, and eased
His wound's imperious anguish : but the blood   840
Came welling from the open gash, and life
Flow'd with the stream : all down his cold white side
The crimson torrent ran, dim now, and soil'd,
Like the soil'd tissue of white violets
Left, freshly gather'd, on their native bank,
By children, whom their nurses call with haste
Indoors from the sun's eye : his head droop'd low,
His limbs grew slack ; motionless, white, he lay—
White, with eyes closed ; only when heavy gasps,
Deep, heavy gasps, quivering through all his frame,   850
Convulsed him back to life, he open'd them,
And fix'd them feebly on his father's face :
Till now all strength was ebb'd, and from his limbs
Unwillingly the spirit fled away,
Regretting the warm mansion which it left,
And youth and bloom, and this delightful world.
    So, on the bloody sand, Sohrab lay dead.
And the great Rustum drew his horseman's cloak
Down o'er his face, and sate by his dead son.
As those black granite pillars, once high-rear'd   860
By Jemshid in Persepolis, to bear
His house, now, mid their broken flights of steps,
Lie prone, enormous, down the mountain side—
So in the sand lay Rustum by his son.
    And night came down over the solemn waste,
And the two gazing hosts, and that sole pair,
And darken'd all ; and a cold fog, with night,

Crept from the Oxus. Soon a hum arose,
As of a great assembly loosed, and fires
Began to twinkle through the fog : for now   870
Both armies moved to camp, and took their meal :
The Persians took it on the open sands
Southward, the Tartars by the river marge :
And Rustum and his son were left alone.

But the majestic river floated on,
Out of the mist and hum of that low land,
Into the frosty starlight, and there moved,
Rejoicing, through the hush'd Chorasmian waste,
Under the solitary moon : he flow'd
Right for the polar star, past Orgunje,   880
Brimming, and bright and large : then sands begin
To hem his watery march, and dam his streams,
And split his currents ; that for many a league
The shorn and parcell'd Oxus strains along
Through beds of sand and matted rushy isles—
Oxus, forgetting the bright speed he had
In his high mountain cradle in Pamere,
A foil'd circuitous wanderer—till at last
The long'd-for dash of waves is heard, and wide
His luminous home of waters opens, bright   890
And tranquil, from whose floor the new-bathed stars
Emerge, and shine upon the Aral Sea.

III.—LONGFELLOW

OSSEO AND OWEENEE

" ONCE, in days no more remembered,
Ages nearer the beginning,
When the heavens were closer to us,
And the Gods were more familiar,
In the North-land lived a hunter,
With ten young and comely daughters,
Tall and lithe as wands of willow ;
Only Oweenee, the youngest,
She the wilful and the wayward,
She the silent, dreamy maiden,   10
Was the fairest of the sisters.

   "All these women married warriors,
Married brave and haughty husbands ;
Only Oweenee, the youngest,
Laughed and flouted all her lovers,
All her young and handsome suitors.
And then married old Osseo,
Old Osseo, poor and ugly,
Broken with age and weak with coughing,
Always coughing like a squirrel.   20

   "Ah, but beautiful within him
Was the spirit of Osseo,
From the Evening Star descended,
Star of Evening, Star of Woman,
Star of tenderness and passion !
All its fire was in his bosom,
All its beauty in his spirit,

All its mystery in his being,
All its splendour in his language !
    "And her lovers, the rejected,   30
Handsome men with belts of wampum.
Handsome men with paint and feathers.
Pointed at her in derision,
Followed her with jest and laughter.
But she said : ' I care not for you,
Care not for your belts of wampum,
Care not for your paint and feathers,
Care not for your jests and laughter ;
I am happy with Osseo ! '
    " Once to some great feast invited,   40
Through the damp and dusk of evening.
Walked together the ten sisters,
Walked together with their husbands ;
Slowly followed old Osseo,
With fair Oweenee beside him ;
All the others chatted gayly,
These two only walked in silence.
    "At the western sky Osseo
Gazed intent, as if imploring,
Often stopped and gazed imploring   50
At the trembling Star of Evening,
At the tender Star of Woman ;
And they heard him murmur softly,
'Ah, showain nemeshin, Nosa !
Pity, pity me, my father ! '
    " ' Listen ! ' said the eldest sister,
' He is praying to his father !
What a pity that the old man
Does not stumble in the pathway,
Does not break his neck by falling ! '   60
And they laughed till all the forest
Rang with their unseemly laughter.

" On their pathway through the woodlands
Lay an oak, by storms uprooted,
Lay the great trunk of an oak-tree,
Buried half in leaves and mosses,
Mouldering, crumbling, huge and hollow
And Osseo, when he saw it,
Gave a shout, a cry of anguish,
Leaped into its yawning cavern.　　　　　　　70
At one end went in an old man,
Wasted, wrinkled, old, and ugly ;
From the other came a young man,
Tall and straight and strong and handsome.

" Thus Osseo was transfigured,
Thus restored to youth and beauty ;
But, alas for good Osseo,
And for Oweenee, the faithful !
Strangely, too, was she transfigured,
Changed into a weak old woman,　　　　　　　80
With a staff she tottered onward,
Wasted, wrinkled, old and ugly !
And the sisters and their husbands
Laughed until the echoing forest
Rang with their unseemly laughter.

" But Osseo turned not from her,
Walked with slower step beside her,
Took her hand, as brown and withered
As an oak-leaf is in Winter,
Called her sweetheart, Nenemoosha,　　　　　　90
Soothed her with soft words of kindness,
Till they reached the lodge of feasting,
Till they sat down in the wigwam,
Sacred to the Star of Evening,
To the tender Star of Woman.

" Wrapt in visions, lost in dreaming,
At the banquet sat Osseo ;

All were merry, all were happy,
All were joyous but Osseo.
Neither food nor drink he tasted,   100
Neither did he speak nor listen,
But as one bewildered sat he,
Looking dreamily and sadly,
First at Oweenee, then upward
At the gleaming sky above them.

   " Then a voice was heard, a whisper,
Coming from the starry distance,
Coming from the empty vastness,
Low, and musical, and tender;
And the voice said : ' O Osseo!   110
O my son, my best beloved!
Broken are the spells that bound you,
All the charms of the magicians,
All the magic powers of evil;
Come to me; ascend, Osseo!

   " ' Taste the food that stands before you:
It is blessed and enchanted,
It has magic virtues in it,
It will change you to a spirit.
All your bowls and all your kettles   120
Shall be wood and clay no longer;
But the bowls be changed to wampum,
And the kettles shall be silver;
They shall shine like shells of scarlet,
Like the fire shall gleam and glimmer.

   " ' And the women shall no longer
Bear the dreary doom of labour,
But be changed to birds, and glisten
With the beauty of the starlight,
Painted with the dusky splendours   130
Of the skies and clouds of evening! '

   " What Osseo heard as whispers,

What as words he comprehended,
Was but music to the others,
Music as of birds afar off,
Of the whippoorwill afar off,
Of the lonely Wawonaissa
Singing in the darksome forest

   "Then the lodge began to tremble,
Straight began to shake and tremble,   140
And they felt it rising, rising,
Slowly through the air ascending,
From the darkness of the tree-tops
Forth into the dewy starlight,
Till it passed the topmost branches ;
And behold ! the wooden dishes
All were changed to shells of scarlet !
And behold ! the earthen kettles
All were changed to bowls of silver !
And the roof-poles of the wigwam   150
Were as glittering rods of silver,
And the roof of bark upon them
As the shining shards of beetles.

   " Then Osseo gazed around him,
And he saw the nine fair sisters,
All the sisters and their husbands,
Changed to birds of various plumage.
Some were jays and some were magpies,
Others thrushes, others blackbirds ;
And they hopped, and sang, and twittered,   160
Perked and fluttered all their feathers,
Strutted in their shining plumage,
And their tails like fans unfolded.

   " Only Oweenee, the youngest,
Was not changed, but sat in silence,
Wasted, wrinkled, old, and ugly,
   Looking sadly at the others ;

Till Osseo, gazing upward,
Gave another cry of anguish,
Such a cry as he had uttered   170
By the oak-tree in the forest.
  " Then returned her youth and beauty,
And her soiled and tattered garments
Were transformed to robes of ermine,
And her staff became a feather,
Yes, a shining silver feather !
  "And again the wigwam trembled,
Swayed and rushed through airy currents,
Through transparent cloud and vapour,
And amid celestial splendours   180
On the Evening Star alighted,
As a snow-flake falls on snow-flake
As a leaf drops on a river,
As the thistle-down on water.
  " Forth with cheerful words of welcome
Came the father of Osseo,
He with radiant locks of silver,
He with eyes serene and tender.
And he said : ' My son, Osseo,
Hang the cage of birds you bring there,   190
Hang the cage with rods of silver,
And the birds with glistening feathers,
At the doorway of my wigwam.'
  "At the door he hung the bird-cage,
And they entered in and gladly
Listened to Osseo's father,
Ruler of the Star of Evening,
As he said : " O my Osseo !
I have had compassion on you,
Given you back your youth and beauty,   200
Into birds of various plumage
Changed your sisters and their husbands ;

Changed them thus because they mocked you
In the figure of an old man,
In that aspect sad and wrinkled,
Could not see your heart of passion,
Could not see your youth immortal;
Only Oweenee, the faithful,
Saw your naked heart and loved you.

" ' In the lodge that glimmers yonder,   210
In the little star that twinkles
Through the vapours, on the left hand,
Lives the envious Evil Spirit,
The Wabeno, the magician,
Who transformed you to an old man.
Take heed lest his beams fall on you,
For the rays he darts around him
Are the power of his enchantment,
Are the arrows that he uses.'

" Many years, in peace and quiet,   220
On the peaceful Star of Evening
Dwelt Osseo with his father;
Many years, in song and flutter,
At the doorway of the wigwam,
Hung the cage with rods of silver.
And fair Oweenee, the faithful,
Bore a son unto Osseo,
With the beauty of his mother,
With the courage of his father.

"And the boy grew up and prospered.   230
And Osseo, to delight him,
Made him little bows and arrows,
Opened the great cage of silver,
And let loose his aunts and uncles,
All those birds with glossy feathers,
For his little son to shoot at.

" Round and round they wheeled and darted,
Filled the Evening Star with music,
With their songs of joy and freedom ;
Filled the Evening Star with splendour, 240
With the fluttering of their plumage ;
Till the boy, the little hunter,
Bent his bow and shot an arrow,
Shot a swift and fatal arrow,
And a bird, with shining feathers,
At his feet fell wounded sorely.

" But, O wondrous transformation !
'Twas no bird he saw before him,
'Twas a beautiful young woman,
With the arrow in her bosom ! 250

" When her blood fell on the planet,
On the sacred Star of Evening,
Broken was the spell of magic,
Powerless was the strange enchantment,
And the youth, the fearless bowman,
Suddenly felt himself descending,
Held by unseen hands, but sinking
Downward through the empty spaces,
Downward through the clouds and vapours,
Till he rested on an island, 260
On an island, green and grassy,
Yonder in the Big-Sea-Water.

"After him he saw descending
All the birds with shining feathers,
Fluttering, falling, wafted downward,
Like the painted leaves of Autumn ;
And the lodge with poles of silver,
With its roof like wings of beetles,
Like the shining shards of beetles,
By the winds of heaven uplifted, 270

Slowly sank upon the island,
Bringing back the good Osseo,
Bringing Oweenee, the faithful.

"Then the birds, again transfigured,
Reassumed the shape of mortals,
Took their shape, but not their stature;
They remained as Little People,
Like the pygmies, the Puk-Wudjies,
And on pleasant nights of Summer,
When the Evening Star was shining,   280
Hand in hand they danced together
On the island's craggy headlands,
On the sand-beach low and level.

"Still their glittering lodge is seen there,
On the tranquil Summer evenings,
And upon the shore the fisher
Sometimes hears their happy voices,
Sees them dancing in the starlight."

IV.—SCOTT

THE BATTLE OF BANNOCKBURN

XIX.

IT was a night of lovely June,
High rode in cloudless blue the moon,
   Demayet smiled beneath her ray;
Old Stirling's towers arose in light,
And, twined in links of silver bright,
   Her winding river lay.
Ah, gentle planet! other sight
Shall greet thee next returning night,
Of broken arms and banners tore,
And marshes dark with human gore,   10
And piles of slaughter'd men and horse,
And Forth that floats the frequent corse,
And many a wounded wretch to plain
Beneath thy silver light in vain!
But now, from England's host, the cry
Thou hear'st of wassail revelry,
While from the Scottish legions pass
The murmur'd prayer, the early mass!—
Here, numbers had presumption given;
There, bands o'er-matched sought aid from Heaven.

XX.

On Gillie's hill, whose height commands   21
The battle-field, fair Edith stands,
With serf and page unfit for war,
To eye the conflict from afar.

O ! with what doubtful agony
She sees the dawning tint the sky !—
Now on the Ochils gleams the sun,
And glistens now Demayet dun ;
Is it the lark that carols shrill ?
   Is it the bittern's early hum ?   30
No !—distant, but increasing still,
The trumpet's sound swells up the hill,
   With the deep murmur of the drum.
Responsive from the Scottish host,
Pipe-clang and bugle-sound were toss'd,
His breast and brow each soldier cross'd,
   And started from the ground ;
Arm'd and array'd for instant fight,
Rose archer, spearman, squire, and knight,
And in the pomp of battle bright   40
   The dread battalia frown'd.

XXI.

Now onward, and in open view,
The countless ranks of England drew,
Dark rolling like the ocean-tide,
When the rough west hath chafed his pride,
And his deep roar sends challenge wide
   To all that bars his way !
In front the gallant archers trode,
The men-at-arms behind them rode,
And midmost of the phalanx broad   50
   The Monarch held his sway.
Beside him many a war-horse fumes,
Around him waves a sea of plumes,
Where many a knight in battle known,
And some who spurs had first braced on,
And deem'd that fight should see them won,
   King Edward's hests obey.

De Argentine attends his side,
With stout De Valence, Pembroke's pride,
Selected champions from the train,   60
To wait upon his bridle-rein.
Upon the Scottish foe he gazed—
—At once, before his sight amazed,
  Sunk banner, spear, and shield ;
Each weapon-point is downward sent,
Each warrior to the ground is bent.
" The rebels, Argentine, repent !
  For pardon they have kneel'd."—
"Aye !—but they bend to other powers,
And other pardon sue than ours !   70
See where yon bare-foot Abbot stands,
And blesses them with lifted hands !
Upon the spot where they have kneel'd,
These men will die, or win the field."—
—" Then prove we if they die or win !
Bid Gloster's Earl the fight begin."

XXII.

Earl Gilbert waved his truncheon high,
  Just as the Northern ranks arose,
Signal for England's archery
  To halt and bend their bows.   80
Then stepp'd each yeoman forth a pace,
Glanced at the intervening space,
  And raised his left hand high ;
To the right ear the cords they bring—
—At once ten thousand bow-strings ring,
  Ten thousand arrows fly !
Nor paused on the devoted Scot
The ceaseless fury of their shot ;
  As fiercely and as fast,

Forth whistling came the gray-goose wing　　90
As the wild hailstones pelt and ring
　　Adown December's blast.
Nor mountain targe of tough bull-hide,
Nor lowland mail, that storm may bide;
Woe, woe to Scotland's banner'd pride,
　　If the fell shower may last!
Upon the right, behind the wood,
Each by his steed dismounted, stood
　　The Scottish chivalry;—
With foot in stirrup, hand on mane,　　100
Fierce Edward Bruce can scarce restrain
His own keen heart, his eager train,
Until the archers gain'd the plain;
　　Then, " Mount, ye gallants free ! "
He cried; and, vaulting from the ground,
His saddle every horseman found.
On high their glittering crests they toss,
As springs the wild-fire from the moss;
The shield hangs down on every breast,
Each ready lance is in the rest,　　110
　　And loud shouts Edward Bruce,—
" Forth, Marshal ! on the peasant foe !
We'll tame the terrors of their bow,
　　And cut the bow-string loose ! "

XXIII.

Then spurs were dash'd in chargers' flanks,
They rush'd among the archer ranks.
No spears were there the shock to let,
No stakes to turn the charge were set,
And how shall yeoman's armour slight,
Stand the long lance and mace of might ?　　120
Or what may their short swords avail,
'Gainst barbed horse and shirt of mail ?

Amid their ranks the chargers sprung,
High o'er their heads the weapons swung,
And shriek and groan the vengeful shout
Give note of triumph and of rout !
Awhile, with stubborn hardihood,
Their English hearts the strife made good.
Borne down at length on every side,
Compell'd to fight, they scatter wide—   130
Let stags of Sherwood leap for glee,
And bound the deer of Dallom-Lee !
The broken bows of Bannock's shore
Shall in the greenwood ring no more !
Round Wakefield's merry May-pole now,
The maids may twine the summer bough,
May northward look with longing glance,
For those that wont to lead the dance,
For the blithe archers look in vain !
Broken, dispersed, in flight o'erta'en,   140
Pierced through, trode down, by thousands slain,
They cumber Bannock's bloody plain.

XXIV.

The King with scorn beheld their flight.
"Are these," he said, " our yeomen wight ?
Each braggart churl could boast before,
Twelve Scottish lives his baldric bore !
Fitter to plunder chase or park,
Than make a manly foe their mark.—
Forward, each gentleman and knight !
Let gentle blood show generous might,   150
And chivalry redeem the fight ! "
To rightward of the wild affray,
The field show'd fair and level way ;
   But, in mid-space, the Bruce's care

Had bored the ground with many a pit,
With turf and brushwood hidden yet,
   That form'd a ghastly snare.
Rushing, ten thousand horsemen came,
With spears in rest, and hearts on flame,
   That panted for the shock !   160
With blazing crests and banners spread,
And trumpet-clang and clamour dread,
The wide plain thunder'd to their tread,
   As far as Stirling rock.
Down ! down ! in headlong overthrow,
Horsemen and horse, the foremost go,
   Wild floundering on the field !
The first are in destruction's gorge,
Their followers wildly o'er them urge ;—
   The knightly helm and shield,   170
The mail, the acton, and the spear,
Strong hand, high heart, are useless here !
Loud from the mass confused the cry
Of dying warriors swells on high,
And steeds that shriek in agony !
They came like mountain-torrent red,
That thunders o'er its rocky bed ;
They broke like that same torrent's wave
When swallow'd by a darksome cave.
Billows on billows burst and boil,   180
Maintaining still the stern turmoil,
And to their wild and tortured groan
Each adds new terrors of his own !

              xxv.

Too strong in courage and in might
Was England yet, to yield the fight.
   Her noblest all are here

Names that to fear were never known,
Bold Norfolk's Earl De Brotherton,
   And Oxford's famed De Vere.
There Gloster plied the bloody sword,   190
And Berkley, Grey, and Hereford,
   Bottetourt and Sanzavere,
Ross, Montague, and Mauley, came,
And Courtenay's pride, and Percy's fame—
Names known too well in Scotland's war,
At Falkirk, Methven, and Dunbar,
Blazed broader yet in after years,
At Cressy red and fell Poitiers.
Pembroke with these, and Argentine,
Brought up the rearward battle-line.   200
With caution o'er the ground they tread,
Slippery with blood and piled with dead,
Till hand to hand in battle set,
The bills with spears and axes met,
And, closing dark on every side,
Raged the full contest far and wide.
Then was the strength of Douglas tried,
Then proved was Randolph's generous pride,
And well did Stewart's actions grace
The sire of Scotland's royal race !   210
   Firmly they kept their ground ;
As firmly England onward press'd,
And down went many a noble crest,
And rent was many a valiant breast,
   And Slaughter revell'd round.

XXVI.

Unflinching foot 'gainst foot was set,
Unceasing blow by blow was met ;
The groans of those who fell

Were drown'd amid the shriller clang
That from the blades and harness rang,   220
   And in the battle-yell.
Yet fast they fell, unheard, forgot,
Both Southern fierce and hardy Scot;
And O! amid that waste of life,
What various motives fired the strife!
The aspiring Noble bled for fame,
The Patriot for his country's claim;
This Knight his youthful strength to prove,
And that to win his lady's love;
Some fought from ruffian thirst of blood,   230
From habit some, or hardihood.
But ruffian stern, and soldier good,
   The noble and the slave,
From various cause the same wild road,
On the same bloody morning, trode,
   To that dark inn, the grave!

XXVII.

The tug of strife to flag begins,
Though neither loses yet nor wins.
High rides the sun, thick rolls the dust,
And feebler speeds the blow and thrust.   240
Douglas leans on his war-sword now,
And Randolph wipes his bloody brow;
Nor less had toil'd each Southern knight,
From morn till mid-day in the fight.
Strong Egremont for air must gasp,
Beauchamp undoes his visor-clasp,
And Montague must quit his spear,
And sinks thy falchion, bold De Vere!
The blows of Berkley fall less fast,
And gallant Pembroke's bugle-blast   250
   Hath lost its lively tone;

Sinks, Argentine, thy battle-word,
And Percy's shout was fainter heard,
   " My merry-men, fight on ! "

XXVIII.

Bruce, with the pilot's wary eye,
The slackening of the storm could spy.
" One effort more, and Scotland's free !
Lord of the Isles, my trust in thee
   Is firm as Ailsa Rock ;
Rush on with Highland sword and targe,   260
I with my Carrick spearmen charge ;
   Now, forward to the shock ! "
At once the spears were forward thrown,
Against the sun the broadswords shone ;
The pibroch lent its maddening tone,
And loud King Robert's voice was known—
" Carrick, press on—they fail ! they fail !
Press on, brave sons of Innisgail,
   The foe is fainting fast !
Each strike for parent, child, and wife,   270
For Scotland, liberty, and life,—
   The battle cannot last ! "

XXIX.

The fresh and desperate onset bore
The foes three furlongs back and more,
Leaving their noblest in their gore.
   Alone, De Argentine
Yet bears on high his red-cross shield,
Gathers the relics of the field,
Renews the ranks where they have reel'd,
   And still makes good the line.   280

C

Brief strife, but fierce,—his efforts raise
A bright but momentary blaze.
Fair Edith heard the Southron shout,
Beheld them turning from the rout,
Heard the wild call their trumpets sent,
In notes 'twixt triumph and lament.
That rallying force, combined anew,
Appear'd in her distracted view,
   To hem the islemen round;
" O God! the combat they renew,   290
   And is no rescue found!
And ye that look thus tamely on,
And see your native land o'erthrown,
O! are your hearts of flesh or stone ? "

XXX.

The multitude that watch'd afar,
Rejected from the ranks of war,
Had not unmoved beheld the fight,
When strove the Bruce for Scotland's right;
Each heart had caught the patriot spark,
Old man and stripling, priest and clerk,   300
Bondsman and serf; even female hand
Stretch'd to the hatchet or the brand;
But, when mute Amadine they heard
Give to their zeal his signal-word,
   A frenzy fired the throng;
" Portents and miracles impeach
Our sloth—the dumb our duties teach—
And he that giveth the mute his speech,
   Can bid the weak be strong.
To us, as to our lords, are given   310
A native earth, a promised heaven;
To us, as to our lords, belongs
The vengeance for our nation's wrongs!

The choice 'twixt death or freedom warms
Our breasts as theirs—To arms, to arms ! "
To arms they flew,—axe, club, or spear,—
And mimic ensigns high they rear,
And, like a banner'd host afar,
Bear down on England's wearied war.

XXXI.

Already scatter'd o'er the plain,   320
Reproof, command, and counsel vain,
The rearward squadrons fled amain,
   Or made but doubtful stay ;
But when they mark'd the seeming show
Of fresh and fierce and marshall'd foe,
   The boldest broke array.
O give their hapless prince his due !
In vain the royal Edward threw
   His person 'mid the spears,
Cried, " Fight ! " to terror and despair,   330
Menaced, and wept, and tore his hair,
   And cursed their caitiff fears ;
Till Pembroke turn'd his bridle rein,
And forced him from the fatal plain.
With them rode Argentine, until
They gain'd the summit of the hill,
   But quitted there the train :—
" In yonder field a gage I left,—
I must not live of fame bereft ;
   I needs must turn again.   340
Speed hence, my Liege, for on your trace
The fiery Douglas takes the chase,
   I know his banner well.
God send my Soverign joy and bliss,
And many a happier field than this !—
   Once more, my Liege, farewell."

XXXII.

Again he faced the battle-field,—
Wildly they fly, are slain, or yield.
" Now then," he said, and couch'd his spear,
" My course is run, the goal is near ;   350
One effort more, one brave career,
    Must close this race of mine."
Then in his stirrups rising high,
He shouted loud his battle-cry,
    " Saint James for Argentine ! "
And, of the bold pursuers, four
The gallant knight from saddle bore ;
But not unharm'd—a lance's point
Has found his breastplate's loosen'd joint,
    An axe has razed his crest ;   360
Yet still on Colonsay's fierce lord,
Who press'd the chase with gory sword,
    He rode with spear in rest,
And through his bloody tartans bored,
    And through his gallant breast.
Nail'd to the earth, the mountaineer
Yet writhed him up against the spear,
    And swung his broadsword round !—
Stirrup, steel-boot, and cuish gave way,
Beneath that blow's tremendous sway,   370
    The blood gush'd from the wound ;
And the grim Lord of Colonsay
    Hath turn'd him on the ground,
And laugh'd in death-pang, that his blade
The mortal thrust so well repaid.

XXXIII.

Now toil'd the Bruce, the battle done,
To use his conquest boldly won ;

And gave command for horse and spear
To press the Southron's scatter'd rear,
Nor let his broken force combine,—   380
When the war-cry of Argentine
   Fell faintly on his ear ;
" Save, save his life," he cried, " O save
   The kind, the noble, and the brave ! "
The squadrons round free passage gave,
   The wounded knight drew near ;
He raised his red-cross shield no more,
Helm, cuish, and breastplate, stream'd with gore,
Yet, as he saw the King advance,
He strove even then to couch his lance—   390
   The effort was in vain !
The spur-stroke fail'd to rouse the horse :
Wounded and weary, in mid course
   He stumbled on the plain.
Then foremost was the generous Bruce
To raise his head, his helm to loose ;—
   " Lord Earl, the day is thine !
My Sovereign's charge, and adverse fate,
Have made our meeting all too late :
   Yet this may Argentine,   400
As boon from ancient comrade, crave,—
A Christian's mass, a soldier's grave."

XXXIV.

Bruce press'd his dying hand—its grasp
Kindly replied ; but, in his clasp,
   It stiffen'd and grew cold—
And, " O farewell ! " the victor cried,
" Of chivalry the flower and pride,
   The arm in battle bold,
The courteous mien, the noble race,
The stainless faith, the manly face !—   410

Bid Ninian's convent light their shrine,
For late-wake of De Argentine.
O'er better knight on death-bier laid,
Torch never gleam'd nor mass was said!"

XXXV.

Not for De Argentine alone,
Through Ninian's church these torches shone,
And rose the death-prayer's awful tone.
That yellow lustre glimmer'd pale,
On broken plate and bloodied mail,
Rent crest and shatter'd coronet,   420
Of Baron, Earl, and Banneret;
And the best names that England knew,
Claim'd in the death-prayer dismal due.
   Yet mourn not, Land of Fame!
Though ne'er the Leopards on thy shield
Retreated from so sad a field,
   Since Norman William came.
Oft may thine annals justly boast
Of battles stern by Scotland lost;
   Grudge not her victory,   430
When for her freeborn rights she strove,
Rights dear to all who freedom love,
   To none so dear as thee!

V.—CRABBE

RICHARD'S WOOING

" Come then, my Brother, now thy tale complete—
I know thy first embarking in the fleet,
Thy entrance in the army, and thy gain
Of plenteous laurels in the wars of Spain,
And what then followed ; but I wish to know
When thou that heart hadst courage to bestow,
When to declare it gain'd, and when to stand
Before the priest, and give the plighted hand ;
So shall I boldness from thy frankness gain
To paint the frenzy that possess'd my brain ;   10
For rather there than in my heart I found
Was my disease ; a poison, not a wound,
A madness, Richard—but, I pray thee, tell
Whom hast thou loved so dearly and so well ? "

The younger man his gentle host obey'd,
For some respect, though not required, was paid,
Perhaps with all that independent pride
Their different states would to the memory glide ;
Yet was his manner unrestrain'd and free,
And nothing in it like servility.   20

Then he began :—When first I reached the land,
I was so ill that death appear'd at hand ;
And though the fever left me, yet I grew
So weak 'twas judged that life would leave me too.

65

I sought a village-priest, my mother's friend,
And I believed with him my days would end :
The man was kind, intelligent, and mild,
Careless and shrewd, yet simple as the child ;
For of the wisdom of the world his share
And mine were equal—neither had to spare ;   30
Else—with his daughters, beautiful and poor—
He would have kept a sailor from his door :
Two then were present, who adorn'd his home,
But ever speaking of a third to come ;
Cheerful they were, not too reserved or free,
I loved them both, and never wish'd them three.

    The Vicar's self, still further to describe,
Was of a simple, but a studious tribe ;
He from the world was distant, not retired,
Nor of it much possess'd, nor much desired :   40
Grave in his purpose, cheerful in his eye,
And with a look of frank benignity.
He much of nature, not of man had seen,
Yet his remarks were often shrewd and keen ;
Taught not by books t' approve or to condemn,
He gain'd but little that he knew from them ;
He read with reverence and respect the few
Whence he his rules and consolations drew.
But men and beasts, and all that lived or moved,
Were books to him ; he studied them and loved.   50
He knew the plants in mountain, wood, or mead ;
He knew the worms that on the foliage feed ;
Knew the small tribes that 'scape the careless eye,
The plant's disease that breeds the embryo-fly ;
And the small creatures who on bark or bough
Enjoy their changes, changed we know not how ;
But now th' imperfect being scarcely moves,
And now takes wing and seeks the sky it loves.

He had no system, and forbore to read
The learned labours of th' immortal Swede ;   60
But smiled to hear the creatures he had known
So long, were now in class and order shown,
Genus and species—" Is it meet," said he,
" This creature's name should one so sounding be ?
'Tis but a fly, though first-born of the spring—
Bombylius majus, dost thou call the thing ?
Majus, indeed ! and yet, in fact, 'tis true,
We all are majors, all are minors too,
Except the first and last,—th' immensely distant two.
And here again—what call the learned this ?   70
Both Hippobosca and Hirundinis ?
Methinks the creature should be proud to find
That he employs the talents of mankind ;
And that his sovreign master shrewdly looks,
Counts all his parts, and puts them in his books.
Well ! go thy way, for I do feel it shame
To stay a being with so proud a name."

Such were his daughters, such my quiet friend
And pleasant was it thus my days to spend ;
But when Matilda at her home I saw,   80
Whom I beheld with anxiousness and awe,
The ease and quiet that I found before
At once departed, and return'd no more.
No more their music soothed me as they play'd,
But soon her words a strong impression made ;
The sweet Enthusiast, so I deem'd her, took
My mind, and fix'd it to her speech and look ;
My soul, dear girl ! she made her constant care,
But never whisper'd to my heart " Beware ! "
In love no dangers rise till we are in the snare.   90

C*

Her father sometimes question'd of my creed,
And seem'd to think it might amendment need ;
But great the difference when the pious maid
To the same errors her attention paid ;
Her sole design that I should think aright,
And my conversion her supreme delight :
Pure was her mind, and simple her intent,
Good all she sought, and kindness all she meant.
Next to religion, friendship was our theme,
Related souls and their refined esteem :   100
We talk'd of scenes where this is real found,
And love subsists without a dart or wound ;
But there intruded thoughts not all serene,
And wishes not so calm would intervene.

" Saw not her father ? "

                Yes ; but saw no more
Than he had seen without a fear before :
He had subsisted by the church and plough,
And saw no cause for apprehension now.
We, too, could live : he thought not passion wrong,
But only wonder'd we delay'd so long.   110

Laugh, if you please, I must my tale pursue—
This sacred friendship thus in secret grew
An intellectual love, most tender, chaste, and true :
Unstain'd, we said, nor knew we how it chanced
To gain some earthly soil as it advanced ;
But yet my friend, and she alone, could prove
How much it differ'd from romantic love—
But this and more I pass—No doubt, at length,
We could perceive the weakness of our strength.

O ! days remember'd well ! remember'd all !   120
The bitter-sweet, the honey and the gall ;

Those garden rambles in the silent night,
Those trees so shady, and that moon so bright ;
That thickset alley by the arbour closed,
That woodbine seat where we at last reposed ;
And then the hopes that came and then were gone,
Quick as the clouds beneath the moon pass'd on :
Now, in this instant, shall my love be shown,
I said—O no, the happy time is flown !

　　You smile : remember, I was weak and low,　　130
And fear'd the passion as I felt it grow :
Will she, I said, to one so poor attend,
Without a prospect, and without a friend ?
I dared not ask her—till a rival came—
But hid the secret, slow-consuming flame.

　　I once had seen him ; then familiar, free,
More than became a common guest to be ;
And sure, I said, he has a look of pride
And inward joy—a lover satisfied.

　　Can you not, Brother, on adventures past,　　140
A thought, as on a lively prospect, cast ?
On days of dear remembrance ! days that seem,
When past—nay, even when present,—like a dream,
These white and blessed days, that softly shine
On few, nor oft on them—have they been thine ?

　　Such days have been—a day of days was one
When, rising gaily with the rising sun,
I took my way to join a happy few,
Known not to me, but whom Matilda knew,
To whom she went a guest, and message sent,　　150
" Come thou to us," and as a guest I went.

There are two ways to Brandon—by the heath
Above the cliff, or on the sand beneath,
Where the small pebbles, wetted by the wave,
To the new day reflected lustre gave :
At first above the rocks I made my way,
Delighted looking at the spacious bay,
And the large fleet that to the northward steer'd
Full sail, that glorious in my view appear'd.

Much as I long'd to see the maid I loved,　　　　160
Through scenes so glorious I at leisure moved ;
For there are times when we do not obey
The master-passion—when we yet delay—
When absence, soon to end, we yet prolong,
And dally with our wish although so strong.

High beat my heart when to the house I came,
And when the ready servant gave my name ;
But when I enter'd that pernicious room,
Gloomy it look'd, and painful was the gloom ;
For there Matilda sat, and her beside　　　　170
That rival soldier, with a soldier's pride ;
With self-approval in his laughing face,
His seem'd the leading spirit of the place :
But, lo ! they rise, and all prepare to take
The promised pleasure on the neighbouring lake.

Good Heaven ! they whisper ! Is it come to this ?
Already !—then may I my doubt dismiss :
Could he so soon a timid girl persuade ?
What rapid progress has the coxcomb made !
And yet how cool her looks, and how demure !　　　　180
The falling snow nor lily's flower so pure :
What can I do ? I must the pair attend,
And watch this horrid business to its end.

There, forth they go ! He leads her to the shore—
Nay, I must follow,—I can bear no more.

O ! you will make me room—'tis very kind,
And meant for him—it tells him he must mind ;
Must not be careless :—I can serve to draw
The soldier on, and keep the man in awe.
O ! I did think she had a guileless heart,   190
Without deceit, capriciousness, or art ;
And yet a stranger, with a coat of red,
Has, by an hour's attention, turn'd her head.

Ah ! how delicious was the morning-drive,
The soul awaken'd, and its hopes alive :
How dull this scene by trifling minds enjoy'd,
The heart in trouble and its hope destroy'd.

Well, now we land—And will he yet support
This part ? What favour has he now to court ?
Favour ! O no ! He means to quit the fair ;   200
How strange ! how cruel ! Will she not despair ?
Well ! take her hand—no further if you please,
I cannot suffer fooleries like these :—
How ? " Love to Julia ! " to his wife ?—O ! dear
And injured creature, how must I appear,
Thus haughty in my looks, and in my words severe ?
Her love to Julia, to the school-day friend
To whom those letters she had lately penn'd !
Can she forgive ? And now I think again,
The man was neither insolent nor vain ;   210
Good humour chiefly would a stranger trace,
Were he impartial, in the air or face ;
And I so splenetic the whole way long,
And she so patient—it was very wrong.

The boat had landed in a shady scene ;
The grove was in its glory, fresh and green ;
The showers of late had swell'd the branch and bough,
And the sun's fervour made them pleasant now.
Hard by an oak arose in all its pride,
And threw its arms along the water's side ;   220
Its leafy limbs, that on the glassy lake
Stretch far, and all those dancing shadows make.

Now must we cross the lake, and as we cross'd
Was my whole soul in sweet emotion lost ;
Clouds in white volumes roll'd beneath the moon,
Softening her light that on the waters shone :
This was such bliss ! even then it seem'd relief
To veil the gladness in a show of grief :
We sigh'd as we conversed, and said, how deep
This lake on which those broad dark shadows sleep ; 230
But here we land, and haply now may choose
Companions home—our way, too, we may lose.

    .   .   .   .   .   .

All thought, yet thinking nothing—all delight
In everything, but nothing in my sight !
Nothing I mark or learn, but am possess'd
Of joys I cannot paint, and I am bless'd
In all that I conceive—whatever is, is best.
Ready to aid all beings, I would go
The world around to succour human woe ;
Yet am so largely happy, that it seems   240
There are no woes, and sorrows are but dreams.

There is a college joy, to scholars known,
When the first honours are proclaim'd their own ;
There is ambition's joy, when in their race
A man surpassing rivals gains his place ;

There is a beauty's joy, amid a crowd
To have that beauty her first fame allow'd ;
And there's the conqueror's joy, when, dubious held
And long the fight, he sees the foe repell'd :

But what are these, or what are other joys,   250
That charm kings, conquerors, beauteous nymphs and
    boys,
Or greater yet, if greater yet be found,
To that delight when love's dear hope is crown'd ?
To the first beating of a lover's heart,
When the loved maid endeavours to impart,
Frankly yet faintly, fondly yet in fear,
The kind confession that he holds so dear.
Now in the morn of our return how strange
Was this new feeling, this delicious change ;
That sweet delirium, when I gazed in fear,   260
That all would yet be lost and disappear.

VI.—WORDSWORTH

MICHAEL

A PASTORAL POEM

If from the public way you turn your steps
Up the tumultuous brook of Green-head Ghyll,
You will suppose that with an upright path
Your feet must struggle ; in such bold ascent
The pastoral mountains front you, face to face.
But, courage ! for around that boisterous brook
The mountains have all opened out themselves,
And made a hidden valley of their own.
No habitation can be seen : but they
Who journey thither find themselves alone   10
With a few sheep, with rocks and stones, and kites
That overhead are sailing in the sky.
It is in truth an utter solitude ;
Nor should I have made mention of this dell
But for one object which you might pass by,
Might see and notice not. Beside the brook
Appears a straggling heap of unhewn stones !
And to that place a story appertains,
Which, though it be ungarnished with events,
Is not unfit, I deem, for the fireside,   20
Or for the summer shade. It was the first
Of those domestic tales that spake to me
Of shepherds, dwellers in the valleys, men
Whom I already loved ;—not verily
For their own sakes, but for the fields and hills

Where was their occupation and abode.
And hence this tale, while I was yet a boy
Careless of books, yet having felt the power
Of nature, by the gentle agency
Of natural objects led me on to feel   30
For passions that were not my own, and think
(At random and imperfectly indeed)
On man, the heart of man, and human life.
Therefore, although it be a history
Homely and rude, I will relate the same
For the delight of a few natural hearts ;
And, with yet fonder feeling, for the sake
Of youthful poets, who among these hills
Will be my second self when I am gone.

    Upon the forest-side in Grasmere Vale   40
There dwelt a shepherd, Michael was his name ;
An old man, stout of heart, and strong of limb.
His bodily frame had been from youth to age
Of unusual strength : his mind was keen,
Intense, and frugal, apt for all affairs,
And in his shepherd's calling he was prompt
And watchful more than ordinary men.
Hence had he learned the meaning of all winds
Of blasts of every tone ; and, oftentimes,
When others heeded not, he heard the south   50
Make subterraneous music, like the noise
Of bagpipers on distant Highland hills.
The shepherd, at such warning, of his flock
Bethought him, and he to himself would say,
" The winds are now devising work for me ! "
And, truly, at all times, the storm—that drives
The traveller to a shelter—summoned him
Up to the mountains : he had been alone
Amid the heart of many thousand mists,

That came to him and left him on the heights.   60
So lived he till his eightieth year was past.
And grossly that man errs, who should suppose
That the green valleys, and the streams and rocks,
Were things indifferent to the shepherd's thoughts.
Fields, where with cheerful spirits he had breathed
The common air ; the hills, which he so oft
Had climbed with vigorous steps ; which had impressed
So many incidents upon his mind
Of hardship, skill or courage, joy or fear ;
Which like a book preserved the memory   70
Of the dumb animals, whom he had saved,
Had fed or sheltered, linking to such acts,
So grateful in themselves, the certainty
Of honourable gain ; these fields, these hills,
Which were his living being, even more
Than his own blood—what could they less ? had laid
Strong hold on his affections, were to him
A pleasurable feeling of blind love,
The pleasure which there is in life itself.

His days had not been passed in singleness.   80
His helpmate was a comely matron, old—
Though younger than himself full twenty years.
She was a woman of a stirring life,
Whose heart was in her house : two wheels she had
Of antique form, this large for spinning wool,
That small for flax ; and if one wheel had rest,
It was because the other was at work.
The pair had but one inmate in their house,
An only child, who had been born to them
When Michael, telling o'er his years, began   90
To deem that he was old,—in shepherd's phrase,
With one foot in the grave. This only son,
With two brave sheep-dogs tried in many a storm,

The one of an inestimable worth,
Made all their household. I may truly say,
That they were as a proverb in the vale
For endless industry. When day was gone,
And from their occupations out of doors
The son and father were come home, even then,
Their labour did not cease ; unless when all   100
Turned to their cleanly supper-board, and there,
Each with a mess of pottage and skimmed milk,
Sat round their basket piled with oaten cakes,
And their plain home-made cheese. Yet when their
    meal
Was ended, Luke (for so the son was named)
And his old father both betook themselves
To such convenient work as might employ
Their hands by the fire-side ; perhaps to card
Wool for the housewife's spindle, or repair
Some injury done to sickle, flail, or scythe,   110
Or other implement of house or field.

    Down from the ceiling by the chimney's edge
That in our ancient uncouth country style
Did with a huge projection overbrow
Large space beneath, and duly as the light
Of day grew dim the housewife hung a lamp ;
An aged utensil, which had performed
Service beyond all others of its kind.
Early at evening did it burn and late,
Surviving comrade of uncounted hours,   120
Which going by from year to year had found
And left the couple neither gay perhaps
Nor cheerful, yet with objects and with hopes,
Living a life of eager industry.
And now, when Luke had reached his eighteenth year
There by the light of this old lamp they sat,

Father and son, while late into the night
The housewife plied her own peculiar work,
Making the cottage through the silent hours
Murmur as with the sound of summer flies.   130
This light was famous in its neighbourhood,
And was a public symbol of the life
The thrifty pair had lived. For, as it chanced,
Their cottage on a plot of rising ground
Stood single, with large prospect, north and south,
High into Easedale up to Dunmail-Raise,
And westward to the village near the lake ;
And from this constant light, so regular
And so far seen, the house itself, by all
Who dwelt within the limits of the vale,   140
Both old and young, was named THE EVENING STAR.

Thus living on through such a length of years,
The shepherd, if he loved himself, must needs
Have loved his helpmate ; but to Michael's heart
This son of his old age was yet more dear—
Less from instinctive tenderness, the same
Blind spirit, which is in the blood of all—
Than that a child, more than all other gifts,
Brings hope with it, and forward-looking thoughts,
And stirrings of inquietude, when they   150
By tendency of nature needs must fail.
Exceeding was the love he bare to him,
His heart and his heart's joy ! For oftentimes
Old Michael, while he was a babe in arms,
Had done him female service, not alone
For pastime and delight, as is the use
Of fathers, but with patient mind enforced
To acts of tenderness ; and he had rocked
His cradle with a woman's gentle hand.

And, in a later time, ere yet the boy   160
Had put on boy's attire, did Michael love,
Albeit of a stern unbending mind,
To have the young one in his sight, when he
Had work by his own door, or when he sat
With sheep before him on his shepherd's stool,
Beneath that large old oak, which near their door
Stood,—and, from its enormous breadth of shade,
Chosen for the shearer's covert from the sun,
Thence in our rustic dialect was called
The CLIPPING TREE, a name which yet it bears.   170
There, while they two were sitting in the shade,
With others round them, earnest all and blithe,
Would Michael exercise his heart with looks
Of fond correction and reproof bestowed
Upon the child, if he disturbed the sheep
By catching at their legs, or with his shouts
Scared them, while they lay still beneath the shears.

And when by Heaven's good grace the boy grew up
A healthy lad, and carried in his cheek
Two steady roses that were five years old,   180
Then Michael from a winter coppice cut
With his own hand a sapling, which he hooped
With iron, making it throughout in all
Due requisites a perfect shepherd's staff,
And gave it to the boy ; wherewith equipt
He as a watchman oftentimes was placed
At gate or gap, to stem or turn the flock ;
And, to his office prematurely called,
There stood the urchin, as you will divine,
Something between a hindrance and a help ;   190
And for this course not always, I believe,
Receiving from his father hire of praise ;

Though nought was left undone which staff or voice
Or looks, or threatening gestures could perform.

But soon as Luke, full ten years old, could stand
Against the mountain blasts ; and to the heights,
Not fearing toil, nor length of weary ways,
He with his father daily went, and they
Were as companions, why should I relate
That objects which the shepherd loved before   200
Were dearer now ? that from the boy there came
Feelings and emanations—things which were
Light to the sun and music to the wind ;
And that the old man's heart seemed born again.
Thus in his father's sight the boy grew up ;
And now when he had reached his eighteenth year.
He was his comfort and his daily hope.

While in this sort the simple household lived
From day to day, to Michael's ear there came
Distressful tidings. Long before the time   210
Of which I speak, the shepherd had been bound
In surety for his brother's son, a man
Of an industrious life, and ample means—
But unforeseen misfortunes suddenly
Had prest upon him,—and old Michael now
Was summoned to discharge the forfeiture,
A grievous penalty, but little less
Than half his substance. This unlooked-for claim
At the first hearing, for a moment took
More hope out of his life than he supposed   220
That any old man ever could have lost.
As soon as he had gathered so much strength
That he could look his trouble in the face
It seemed that his sole refuge was to sell
A portion of his patrimonial fields,
Such was his first resolve ; he thought again,

And his heart failed him. " Isabel," said he,
Two evenings after he had heard the news,
" I have been toiling more than seventy years,
And in the open sunshine of God's love   230
Have we all lived ; yet if these fields of ours
Should pass into a stranger's hand, I think
That I could not lie quiet in my grave.
Our lot is a hard lot ; the sun himself
Has scarcely been more diligent than I ;
And I have lived to be a fool at last
To my own family. An evil man
That was, and made an evil choice, if he
Were false to us ; and if he were not false,
There are ten thousand to whom loss like this   240
Had been no sorrow. I forgive him—but
'Twere better to be dumb than to talk thus.

When I began, my purpose was to speak
Of remedies and of a cheerful hope.
Our Luke shall leave us, Isabel ; the land
Shall not go from us, and it shall be free ;
He shall possess it free as is the wind
That passes over it. We have, thou knowest,
Another kinsman—he will be our friend
In this distress. He is a prosperous man,   250
Thriving in trade—and Luke to him shall go,
And with his kinsman's help and his own thrift
He quickly will repair this loss, and then
May come again to us. If here he stay,
What can be done ? Where every one is poor,
What can be gained ? " At this the old man paused,
And Isabel sat silent, for her mind
Was busy, looking back into past times.
There's Richard Bateman, thought she to herself,
He was a parish-boy—at the church-door   260
They made a gathering for him, shillings, pence,

And halfpennies, wherewith the neighbours bought
A basket, which they filled with pedlar's wares ;
And with this basket on his arm, the lad
Went up to London, found a master there,
Who out of many chose the trusty boy
To go and overlook his merchandise
Beyond the seas : where he grew wondrous rich,
And left estates and moneys to the poor,
And at his birthplace built a chapel floored   270
With marble, which he sent from foreign lands.
These thoughts, and many others of like sort,
Passed quickly through the mind of Isabel
And her face brightened. The old man was glad
And thus resumed :—" Well, Isabel ! this scheme
These two days has been meat and drink to me,
Far more than we have lost is left us yet.
We have enough—I wish indeed that I
Were younger,—but this hope is a good hope.
Make ready Luke's best garments, of the best   280
Buy for him more, and let us send him forth
To-morrow, or the next day, or to-night ;
If he *could* go, the boy should go to-night."
Here Michael ceased, and to the fields went forth
With light heart. The housewife for five days
Was restless morn and night, and all day long
Wrought on with her best fingers to prepare
Things needful for the journey of her son.
But Isabel was glad when Sunday came
To stop her in her work : for, when she lay   290
By Michael's side, she through the two last nights
Heard him, how he was troubled in his sleep :
And when they rose at morning she could see
That all his hopes were gone. That day at noon
She said to Luke, while they two by themselves
Were sitting at the door, " Thou must not go :

We have no other child but thee to lose,
None to remember—do not go away,
For if thou leave thy father he will die."
The youth made answer with a jocund voice ;   300
And Isabel, when she had told her fears,
Recovered heart. That evening her best fare
Did she bring forth, and all together sat
Like happy people round a Christmas fire.

   With daylight Isabel resumed her work ;
And all the ensuing week the house appeared
As cheerful as a grove in spring : at length
The expected letter from their kinsman came,
With kind assurances that he would do
His utmost for the welfare of the boy ;   310
To which, requests were added, that forthwith
He might be sent to him. Ten times or more
The letter was read over ; Isabel
Went forth to show it to the neighbours round ;
Nor was there at that time on English land
A prouder heart than Luke's. When Isabel
Had to her house returned, the old man said,
" He shall depart to-morrow." To this word
The housewife answered, talking much of things
Which, if at such short notice he should go,   320
Would surely be forgotten. But at length
She gave consent, and Michael was at ease.

   Near the tumultuous brook of Green-head Ghyll,
In that deep valley, Michael had designed
To build a sheep-fold ; and, before he heard
The tidings of his melancholy loss,
For this same purpose he had gathered up
A heap of stones, which by the streamlet's edge
Lay thrown together, ready for the work.

With Luke that evening thitherward he walked ;   330
And soon as they had reached the place he stopped,
And thus the old man spake to him.—" My son,
To-morrow thou wilt leave me : with full heart
I look upon thee, for thou art the same
That wert a promise to me ere thy birth,
And all thy life hast been my daily joy.
I will relate to thee some little part
Of our two histories ; 'twill do thee good
When thou art from me, even if I should speak
Of things thou canst not know of.——After thou   340
First cam'st into the world—as oft befalls
To new-born infants—thou didst sleep away
Two days, and blessings from thy father's tongue
Then fell upon thee. Day by day passed on,
And still I loved thee with increasing love.
Never to living ear came sweeter sounds
Than when I heard thee by our own fireside
First uttering, without words, a natural tune ;
When thou, a feeding babe, didst in thy joy
Sing at thy mother's breast. Month followed month, 350
And in the open fields my life was passed
And on the mountains, else I think that thou
Hadst been brought up upon thy father's knees.
But we were playmates, Luke : among these hills,
As well thou know'st, in us the old and young
Have played together, nor with me didst thou
Lack any pleasure which a boy can know."
Luke had a manly heart ; but at these words
He sobbed aloud. The old man grasped his hand,
And said, " Nay, do not take it so—I see   360
That these are things of which I need not speak.
Even to the utmost I have been to thee
A kind and good father : and herein
I but repay a gift which I myself

Received at others' hands ; for, though now old
Beyond the common life of man, I still
Remember them who loved me in my youth.
Both of them sleep together : here they lived
As all their forefathers had done ; and when
At length their time was come, they were not loath 370
To give their bodies to the family mould.
I wished that thou shouldst live the life they lived.
But 'tis a long time to look back, my son,
And see so little gain from threescore years.
These fields were burthened when they came to me ;
Till I was forty years of age, not more
Than half of my inheritance was mine.
I toiled and toiled ; God blessed me in my work,
And till these three weeks past the land was free.
It looks as if it never could endure   380
Another master. Heaven forgive me, Luke,
If I judge ill for thee, but it seems good
That thou shouldst go." At this the old man paused ;
Then, pointing to the stones near which they stood,
Thus, after a short silence, he resumed :
" This was a work for us ; and now, my son,
It is a work for me. But, lay one stone—
Here, lay it for me, Luke, with thine own hands.
Nay, boy, be of good hope ;—we both may live
To see a better day. At eighty-four   390
I still am strong and hale ;—do thou thy part,
I will do mine.—I will begin again
With many tasks that were resigned to thee ;
Up to the heights, and in among the storms,
Will I without thee go again, and do
All works which I was wont to do alone,
Before I knew thy face.—Heaven bless thee, boy !
Thy heart these two weeks has been beating fast

With many hopes—It should be so—Yes—yes—
I knew that thou couldst never have a wish   400
To leave me, Luke : thou hadst been bound to me
Only by links of love : when thou art gone,
What will be left to us !—But, I forget
My purposes. Lay now the corner-stone,
As I requested ; and hereafter, Luke,
When thou art gone away, should evil men
Be thy companions, think of me, my son,
And of this moment ; hither turn thy thoughts,
And God will strengthen thee : amid all fear
And all temptation, Luke, I pray that thou   410
Mayst bear in mind the life thy fathers lived,
Who, being innocent, did for that cause
Bestir them in good deeds. Now, fare thee well—
When thou return'st, thou in this place wilt see
A work which is not here : a covenant
'Twill be between us——But, whatever fate
Befall thee, I shall love thee to the last,
And bear thy memory with me to the grave."

       The shepherd ended here ; and Luke stooped down,
And, as his father had requested, laid   420
The first stone of the sheep-fold. At the sight
The old man's grief broke from him ; to his heart
He pressed his son, he kisséd him and wept ;
And to the house together they returned.
Hushed was that house in peace, or seeming peace,
Ere the night fell ;—with morrow's dawn the boy
Began his journey, and when he had reached
The public way, he put on a bold face ;
And all the neighbours as he passed their doors
Came forth with wishes and with farewell prayers,   430
That followed him till he was out of sight.

A good report did from their kinsman come,
Of Luke and his well-doing : and the boy
Wrote loving letters, full of wondrous news,
Which, as the housewife phrased it, were throughout
" The prettiest letters that were ever seen."
Both parents read them with rejoicing hearts.
So, many months passed on : and once again
The shepherd went about his daily work
With confident and cheerful thoughts ; and now   440
Sometimes when he could find a leisure hour
He to that valley took his way, and there
Wrought at the sheep-fold. Meantime Luke began
To slacken in his duty ; and at length
He in the dissolute city gave himself
To evil courses : ignominy and shame
Fell on him, so that he was driven at last
To seek a hiding-place beyond the seas.

There is a comfort in the strength of love ;
'Twill make a thing endurable, which else   450
Would overset the brain, or break the heart :
I have conversed with more than one who well
Remember the old man, and what he was
Years after he had heard this heavy news.
His bodily frame had been from youth to age
Of an unusual strength. Among the rocks
He went, and still looked up upon the sun,
And listened to the wind ; and as before
Performed all kinds of labour for his sheep,
And for the land his small inheritance.   460
And to that hollow dell from time to time
Did he repair, to build the fold of which
His flock had need. 'Tis not forgotten yet
The pity which was then in every heart
For the old man—and 'tis believed by all

That many and many a day he thither went,
And never lifted up a single stone.

There, by the sheep-fold, sometimes was he seen
Sitting alone, with that his faithful dog,
Then old, beside him, lying at his feet.   470
The length of full seven years from time to time
He at the building of this sheep-fold wrought,
And left the work unfinished when he died.
Three years, or little more, did Isabel
Survive her husband : at her death the estate
Was sold, and went into a stranger's hand.
The cottage which was named THE EVENING STAR
Is gone—the ploughshare has been through the ground
On which it stood ; great changes have been wrought
In all the neighbourhood :—yet the oak is left   480
That grew beside their door ; and the remains
Of the unfinished sheep-fold may be seen
Beside the boisterous brook of Green-head Ghyll.

VII.—WILLIAM MORRIS

ATALANTA'S RACE

I.

Upon the shore of Argolis there stands
A temple to the goddess that he sought,
That, turned unto the lion-bearing lands,
Fenced from the east, of cold winds hath no thought,
Though to no homestead there the sheaves are brought,
No groaning press torments the close-clipped murk,
Lonely the fane stands, far from all men's work.

II.

Pass through a close, set thick with myrtle-trees,
Through the brass doors that guard the holy place,
And entering, hear the washing of the seas
That twice a-day rise high above the base,
And with the south-west urging them, embrace
The marble feet of her that standeth there
That shrink not, naked though they be and fair.

III.

Small is the fane through which the sea-wind sings
About Queen Venus' well-wrought image white,
But hung around are many precious things,
The gifts of those who, longing for delight,
Have hung them there within the goddess' sight,
And in return have taken at her hands
The living treasures of the Grecian lands.

IV.

And thither now has come Milanion,
And showed unto the priests' wide open eyes
Gifts fairer than all those that there have shone,
Silk cloths, inwrought with Indian fantasies,
And bowls inscribed with sayings of the wise
Above the deeds of foolish living things,
And mirrors fit to be the gifts of kings.

V.

And now before the Sea-born One he stands,
By the sweet veiling smoke made dim and soft,
And while the incense trickles from his hands,
And while the odorous smoke-wreaths hang aloft,
Thus doth he pray to her : " O Thou, who oft
Hast holpen man and maid in their distress,
Despise me not for this my wretchedness !

VI.

" O goddess, among us who dwell below,
Kings and great men, great for a little while,
Have pity on the lowly heads that bow,
Nor hate the hearts that love them without guile ;
Wilt thou be worse than these, and is thy smile
A vain device of him who set thee here,
An empty dream of some artificer ?

VII.

" O, great one, some men love, and are ashamed ;
Some men are weary of the bonds of love ;
Yea, and by some men lightly art thou blamed,

That from thy toils their lives they cannot move,
And 'mid the ranks of men their manhood prove.
Alas ! O goddess, if thou slayest me
What new immortal can I serve but thee ?

VIII.

" Think then, will it bring honour to thy head
If folk say, ' Everything aside he cast
And to all fame and honour was he dead,
And to his one hope now is dead at last,
Since all unholpen he is gone and past :
Ah, the gods love not man, for certainly,
He to his helper did not cease to cry.'

IX.

" Nay, but thou wilt help ; they who died before
Not single-hearted as I deem came here,
Therefore unthanked they laid their gifts before
Thy stainless feet, still shivering with their fear,
Lest in their eyes their true thought might appear,
Who sought to be the lords of that fair town,
Dreaded of men and winners of renown.

X.

" O Queen, thou knowest I pray not for this :
O set us down together in some place
Where not a voice can break our heaven of bliss,
Where nought but rocks and I can see her face,
Softening beneath the marvel of thy grace,
Where not a foot our vanished steps can track—
The golden age, the golden age come back !

D

XI.

" O fairest, hear me now who do thy will,
Plead for thy rebel that she be not slain,
But live and love and be thy servant still ;
Ah, give her joy and take away my pain,
And thus two long-enduring servants gain.
An easy thing this is to do for me,
What need of my vain words to weary thee !

XII.

" But none the less, this place will I not leave
Until I needs must go my death to meet,
Or at thy hands some happy sign receive
That in great joy we twain may one day greet
Thy presence here and kiss thy silver feet,
Such as we deem thee, fair beyond all words,
Victorious o'er our servants and our lords."

XIII.

Then from the altar back a space he drew,
But from the Queen turned not his face away,
But 'gainst a pillar leaned, until the blue
That arched the sky, at ending of the day,
Was turned to ruddy gold and changing grey,
And clear, but low, the nigh-ebbed windless sea
In the still evening murmured ceaselessly.

XIV.

And there he stood when all the sun was down,
Nor had he moved, when the dim golden light,
Like the far lustre of a godlike town,

Had left the world to seeming hopeless night,
Nor would he move the more when wan moonlight
Streamed through the pillars for a little while,
And lighted up the white Queen's changeless smile.

xv.

Nought noted he the shallow-flowing sea
As step by step it set the wrack a-swim,
The yellow torchlight nothing noted he
Wherein with fluttering gown and half-bared limb
The temple damsels sung their midnight hymn,
And nought the doubled stillness of the fane
When they were gone and all was hushed again.

xvi.

But when the waves had touched the marble base,
And steps the fish swim over twice a-day,
The dawn beheld him sunken in his place
Upon the floor ; and sleeping there he lay,
Not heeding aught the little jets of spray
The roughened sea brought nigh, across him cast,
For as one dead all thought from him had passed.

xvii.

Yet long before the sun had showed his head,
Long ere the varied hangings on the wall
Had gained once more their blue and green and red,
He rose as one some well-known sign doth call
When war upon the city's gates doth fall,
And scarce like one fresh risen out of sleep,
He 'gan again his broken watch to keep.

XVIII.

Then he turned round ; not for the sea-gull's cry
That wheeled above the temple in his flight,
Not for the fresh south wind that lovingly
Breathed on the new-born day and dying night,
But some strange hope 'twixt fear and great delight
Drew round his face, now flushed, now pale and wan,
And still constrained his eyes the sea to scan.

XIX.

Now a faint light lit up the southern sky,
Not sun nor moon, for all the world was grey,
But this a bright cloud seemed, that drew anigh,
Lighting the dull waves that beneath it lay
As towards the temple still it took its way,
And still grew greater, till Milanion
Saw nought for dazzling light that round him shone.

XX.

But as he staggered with his arms outspread,
Delicious unnamed odours breathed around,
For languid happiness he bowed his head,
And with wet eyes sank down upon the ground,
Nor wished for aught, nor any dream he found
To give him reason for that happiness,
Or make him ask more knowledge of his bliss.

XXI.

At last his eyes were cleared, and he could see
Through happy tears the goddess face to face
With that faint image of Divinity,

Whose well-wrought smile and dainty changeless grace
Until that morn so gladdened all the place ;
Then he, unwitting, cried aloud her name
And covered up his eyes for fear and shame.

XXII.

But through the stillness he her voice could hear
Piercing his heart with joy scarce bearable,
That said, " Milanion, wherefore dost thou fear ?
I am not hard to those who love me well ;
List to what I a second time will tell,
And thou mayest hear perchance, and live to save
The cruel maiden from a loveless grave.

XXIII.

" See, by my feet three golden apples lie—
Such fruit among the heavy roses falls,
Such fruit my watchful damsels carefully
Store up within the best loved of my walls,
Ancient Damascus, where the lover calls
Above my unseen head, and faint and light
The rose-leaves flutter round me in the night.

XXIV.

"And note, that these are not alone most fair
With heavenly gold, but longing strange they bring
Unto the hearts of men, who will not care,
Beholding these, for any once-loved thing
Till round the shining sides their fingers cling.
And thou shalt see thy well-girt swiftfoot maid,
By sight of these amidst her glory stayed.

XXV.

" For bearing these within a scrip with thee,
When first she heeds thee from the starting-place
Cast down the first one for her eyes to see,
And when she turns aside make on apace,
And if again she heads thee in the race
Spare not the other two to cast aside
If she not long enough behind will bide.

XXVI.

" Farewell, and when has come the happy time
That she Diana's raiment must unbind
And all the world seems blessed with Saturn's clime
And thou with eager arms about her twined
Beholdest first her grey eyes growing kind,
Surely, O trembler, thou shalt scarcely then
Forget the Helper of unhappy men."

XXVII.

Milanion raised his head at this last word,
For now so soft and kind she seemed to be
No longer of her Godhead was he feared ;
Too late he looked, for nothing could he see
But the white image glimmering doubtfully
In the departing twilight cold and grey,
And those three apples on the steps that lay.

XXVIII.

These then he caught up quivering with delight,
Yet fearful lest it all might be a dream,
And though aweary with the watchful night,

And sleepless nights of longing, still did deem
He could not sleep ; but yet the first sunbeam
That smote the fane across the heaving deep
Shone on him laid in calm untroubled sleep.

XXIX.

But little ere the noontide did he rise,
And why he felt so happy scarce could tell
Until the gleaming apples met his eyes.
Then leaving the fair place where this befell
Oft he looked back as one who loved it well,
Then homeward to the haunts of men 'gan wend
To bring all things unto a happy end.

XXX.

Now has the lingering month at last gone by,
Again are all folk round the running place,
Nor other seems the dismal pageantry
Than heretofore, but that another face
Looks o'er the smooth course ready for the race,
For now, beheld of all, Milanion
Stands on the spot he twice has looked upon.

XXXI.

But yet—what change is this that holds the maid ?
Does she indeed see in his glittering eye
More than disdain of the sharp shearing blade,
Some happy hope of help and victory ?
The others seemed to say, " We come to die,
Look down upon us for a little while,
That dead, we may bethink us of thy smile."

MORRIS

XXXII.

But he—what look of mastery was this
He cast on her ? why were his lips so red ?
Why was his face so flushed with happiness ?
So looks not one who deems himself but dead,
E'en if to death he bows a willing head ;
So rather looks a god well pleased to find
Some earthly damsel fashioned to his mind.

XXXIII.

Why must she drop her lids before his gaze,
And even as she casts adown her eyes
Redden to note his eager glance of praise,
And wish that she were clad in other guise ?
Why must the memory to her heart arise
Of things unnoticed when they first were heard,
Some lover's song, some answering maiden's word ?

XXXIV.

What makes these longings, vague, without a name,
And this vain pity never felt before,
This sudden languor, this contempt of fame,
This tender sorrow for the time past o'er,
These doubts that grow each minute more and more ?
Why does she tremble as the time grows near,
And weak defeat and woeful victory fear

XXXV.

Now while she seemed to hear her beating heart,
Above their heads the trumpet blast rang out
And forth they sprang ; and she must play her part.

Then flew her white feet, knowing not a doubt,
Though slackening once, she turned her head about,
But then she cried aloud and faster fled
Than e'er before, and all men deemed him dead.

XXXVI.

But with no sound he raised aloft his hand,
And thence what seemed a ray of light there flew
And past the maid rolled on along the sand ;
Then trembling she her feet together drew
And in her heart a strong desire there grew
To have the toy ; some god she thought had given
That gift to her, to make of earth a heaven.

XXXVII.

Then from the course with eager steps she ran,
And in her odorous bosom laid the gold.
But when she turned again, the great-limbed man,
Now well ahead she failed not to behold,
And mindful of her glory waxing cold,
Sprang up and followed him in hot pursuit,
Though with one hand she touched the golden fruit.

XXXVIII.

Note too, the bow that she was wont to bear
She laid aside to grasp the glittering prize,
And o'er her shoulder from the quiver fair
Three arrows fell and lay before her eyes
Unnoticed, as amidst the people's cries
She sprang to head the strong Milanion,
Who now the turning-post had well-nigh won.

D*

XXXIX.

But as he set his mighty hand on it
White fingers underneath his own were laid,
And white limbs from his dazzled eyes did flit,
Then he the second fruit cast by the maid:
She ran awhile, and then as one afraid
Wavered and stopped, and turned and made no stay,
Until the globe with its bright fellow lay.

XL.

Then, as a troubled glance she cast around
Now far ahead the Argive could she see,
And in her garment's hem one hand she wound
To keep the double prize, and strenuously
Sped o'er the course, and little doubt had she
To win the day, though now but scanty space
Was left betwixt him and the winning place.

XLI.

Short was the way unto such winged feet,
Quickly she gained upon him till at last
He turned about her eager eyes to meet
And from his hand the third fair apple cast.
She wavered not, but turned and ran so fast
After the prize that should her bliss fulfil,
That in her hand it lay ere it was still.

XLII.

Nor did she rest, but turned about to win
Once more, an unblest woeful victory—
And yet—and yet—why does her breath begin

To fail her, and her feet drag heavily ?
Why fails she now to see if far or nigh
The goal is ? why do her grey eyes grow dim ?
Why do these tremors run through every limb ?

XLIII.

She spreads her arms abroad some stay to find
Else must she fall, indeed, and findeth this,
A strong man's arms about her body twined.
Nor may she shudder now to feel his kiss,
So wrapped she is in new unbroken bliss :
Made happy that the foe the prize hath won,
She weeps glad tears for all her glory done.

VIII.—KEATS

THE EVE OF ST. AGNES

I.

St. Agnes' Eve—Ah, bitter chill it was !
The owl, for all his feathers, was a-cold ;
The hare limped trembling through the frozen grass,
And silent was the flock in woolly fold :
Numb were the Beadsman's fingers, while he told
His rosary, and while his frosted breath,
Like pious incense from a censer old,
Seemed taking flight for heaven, without a death,
Past the sweet Virgin's picture, while his prayer he saith.

II.

His prayer he saith, this patient, holy man ;
Then takes his lamp, and riseth from his knees,
And back returneth, meagre, barefoot, wan,
Along the chapel aisle by slow degrees :
The sculptured dead, on each side, seem to freeze,
Imprisoned in black, purgatorial rails :
Knights, ladies, praying in dumb orat'ries,
He passeth by ; and his weak spirit fails
To think how they may ache in icy hoods and mails.

III.

Northward he turneth through a little door,
And scarce three steps, ere Music's golden tongue
Flattered to tears this aged man and poor ;
But no—already had his death-bell rung ;

The joys of all his life were said and sung :
His was harsh penance on St. Agnes' Eve :
Another way he went, and soon among
Rough ashes sat he for his soul's reprieve,
And all night kept awake, for sinners' sake to grieve.

IV.

That ancient Beadsman heard the prelude soft ;
And so it chanced, for many a door was wide,
From hurry to and fro. Soon, up aloft,
The silver, snarling trumpets 'gan to chide :
The level chambers, ready with their pride,
Were glowing to receive a thousand guests :
The carved angels, ever eager-eyed,
Stared, where upon their heads the cornice rests,
With hair blown back, and wings put cross-wise on their
    breasts.

V.

At length burst in the argent revelry,
With plume, tiara, and all rich array,
Numerous as shadows haunting fairily
The brain, new stuffed in youth, with triumphs gay
Of old romance. These let us wish away,
And turn, sole thoughted, to one lady there,
Whose heart had brooded, all that wintry day,
On love, and winged St. Agnes' saintly care,
As she had heard old dames full many times declare.

VI.

They told her how, upon St. Agnes' Eve,
Young virgins might have visions of delight,
And soft adorings from their loves receive
Upon the honeyed middle of the night,

If ceremonies due they did aright ;
As, supperless to bed they must retire,
And couch supine their beauties, lily white ;
Nor look behind, nor sideways, but require
Of Heaven with upward eyes for all that they desire.

VII.

Full of this whim was thoughtful Madeline :
The music, yearning like a God in pain,
She scarcely heard : her maiden eyes divine
Fixed on the floor, saw many a sweeping train
Pass by—she heeded not at all : in vain
Came many a tiptoe, amorous cavalier,
And back retired, not cooled by high disdain ;
But she saw not : her heart was otherwhere :
She sighed for Agnes' dreams, the sweetest of the year.

VIII.

She danced along with vague, regardless eyes,
Anxious her lips, her breathing quick and short :
The hallowed hour was near at hand : she sighs
Amid the timbrels, and the thronged resort
Of whisperers in anger, or in sport ;
'Mid looks of love, defiance, hate, and scorn,
Hoodwinked with fairy fancy : all amort,
Save to St. Agnes and her lambs unshorn,
And all the bliss to be before to-morrow morn.

IX.

So, purposing each moment to retire,
She lingered still. Meantime, across the moors,
Had come young Porphyro, with heart on fire
For Madeline.   Beside the portal doors.

Buttressed from moonlight, stands he, and implores
All saints to give him sight of Madeline,
But for one moment in the tedious hours,
That he might gaze and worship all unseen ;
Perchance speak, kneel, touch, kiss—in sooth such things
    have been.

x.

He ventures in : let no buzzed whisper tell :
All eyes be muffled, or a hundred swords
Will storm his heart, Love's fev'rous citadel :
For him, those chambers held barbarian hordes,
Hyena foemen, and hot-blooded lords,
Whose very dogs would execrations howl
Against his lineage : not one breast affords
Him any mercy, in that mansion foul,
Save one old beldame, weak in body and in soul.

xi.

Ah, happy chance ! the agèd creature came,
Shuffling along with ivory-headed wand,
To where he stood, hid from the torch's flame,
Behind a broad hall-pillar, far beyond
The sound of merriment and chorus bland :
He startled her ; but soon she knew his face,
And grasped his fingers in her palsied hand,
    Saying, " Mercy, Porphyro ! hie thee from this place ;
They are all here to-night, the whole bloodthirsty race !

xii.

" Get hence ! get hence ! there's dwarfish Hildebrand ;
He had a fever late, and in the fit
He cursèd thee and thine, both house and land :
Then there's that old Lord Maurice, not a whit

More tame for his grey hairs—Alas me ! flit !
Flit like a ghost away."—"Ah, gossip dear,
We're safe enough ; here in this armchair sit,
And tell me how"—" Good Saints ! not here, not here;
Follow me, child, or else these stones will be thy bier."

XIII.

He followed through a lowly archèd way,
Brushing the cobwebs with his lofty plume,
And as she muttered, " Well-a—well-a-day ! "
He found him in a little moonlight room,
Pale, latticed, chill, and silent as a tomb.
" Now tell me where is Madeline," said he,
" O tell me, Angela, by the holy loom
Which none but secret sisterhood may see,
When they St. Agnes' wool are weaving piously."

XIV.

" St. Agnes ! Ah ! it is St. Agnes' Eve—
Yet men will murder upon holy days :
Thou must hold water in a witch's sieve,
And be liege-lord of all the Elves and Fays,
To venture so : it fills me with amaze
To see thee, Porphyro !—St. Agnes' Eve !
God's help ! my lady fair the conjuror plays
This very night : good angels her deceive !
But let me laugh awhile, I've mickle time to grieve."

XV.

Feebly she laughèd in the languid moon,
While Porphyro upon her face doth look,
Like puzzled urchin on an agèd crone
Who keepeth closed a wondrous riddle-book,

As spectacled she sits in chimney-nook.
But soon his eyes grew brilliant, when she told
His lady's purpose ; and he scarce could brook
Tears, at the thought of those enchantments cold,
And Madeline asleep in lap of legends old.

XVI.

Sudden a thought came like a full-blown rose,
Flushing his brow, and in his painèd heart
Made purple riot : then doth he propose
A stratagem, that makes the beldame start :
" A cruel man and impious thou art :
Sweet lady, let her pray, and sleep, and dream
Alone with her good angels, far apart
From wicked men like thee. Go, go !—I deem
Thou canst not surely be the same that thou didst seem."

XVII.

" I will not harm her, by all saints I swear,"
Quoth Porphyro : " O may I ne'er find grace
When my weak voice shall whisper its last prayer,
If one of her soft ringlets I displace,
Or look with ruffian passion in her face ;
Good Angela, believe me by these tears ;
Or I will, even in a moment's space,
Awake, with horrid shout, my foemen's ears,
And beard them, though they be more fanged than wolves
        and bears."

XVIII.

"Ah ! why wilt thou affright a feeble soul ?
A poor, weak, palsy-stricken, churchyard thing,
Whose passing-bell may ere the midnight toll ;
Whose prayers for thee, each morn and evening,

Were never missed." Thus plaining, doth she bring
A gentler speech from burning Porphyro ;
So woeful, and of such deep sorrowing,
That Angela gives promise she will do
Whatever he shall wish, betide her weal or woe.

XIX.

Which was, to lead him, in close secrecy,
Even to Madeline's chamber, and there hide
Him in a closet, of such privacy
That he might see her beauty unespied,
And win perhaps that night a peerless bride.
While legioned fairies paced the coverlet,
And pale enchantment held her sleepy-eyed.
Never on such a night have lovers met,
Since Merlin paid his Demon all the monstrous debt.

XX.

" It shall be as thou wishest," said the Dame :
"All cates and dainties shall be storèd there
Quickly on this feast night : by the tambour-frame
Her own lute thou wilt see : no time to spare,
For I am slow and feeble, and scarce dare
On such a catering trust my dizzy head.
Wait here, my child, with patience ; kneel in prayer
The while : Ah ! thou must needs the lady wed,
Or may I never leave my grave among the dead."

XXI.

So saying, she hobbled off with busy fear.
The lover's endless minutes slowly passed ;
The dame returned, and whispered in his ear
To follow her ; with agèd eyes aghast

From fright of dim espial. Safe at last,
Through many a dusky gallery, they gain
The maiden's chamber, silken, hushed, and chaste ;
Where Porphyro took covert, pleased amain.
His poor guide hurried back with agues in her brain.

XXII.

Her falt'ring hand upon the balustrade,
Old Angela was feeling for the stair,
When Madeline, St. Agnes' charmèd maid,
Rose, like a missioned spirit, unaware :
With silver taper's light, and pious care,
She turned, and down the agèd gossip led
To a safe level matting. Now prepare,
Young Porphyro, for gazing on that bed ;
She comes, she comes again, like ringdove frayed and fled.

XXIII.

Out went the taper as she hurried in ;
Its little smoke, in pallid moonshine, died :
She closed the door, she panted, all akin
To spirits of the air, and visions wide :
No uttered syllable, or, woe betide !
But to her heart, her heart was voluble,
Paining with eloquence her balmy side ;
As though a tongueless nightingale should swell
Her throat in vain, and die, heart-stifled, in her dell.

XXIV.

A casement high and triple-arched there was,
All garlanded with carven imag'ries
Of fruits, and flowers, and bunches of knot-grass,
And diamonded with panes of quaint device,

Innumerable of stains and splendid dyes,
As are the tiger-moth's deep-damasked wings;
And in the midst, 'mong thousand heraldries,
And twilight saints, and dim emblazonings,
A shielded scutcheon blushed with blood of queens and
    kings.

XXV.

Full on this casement shone the wintry moon,
And threw warm gules on Madeline's fair breast,
As down she knelt for heaven's grace and boon;
Rose-bloom fell on her hands, together prest,
And on her silver cross soft amethyst,
And on her hair a glory, like a saint:
She seemed a splendid angel, newly drest,
Save wings, for heaven:—Porphyro grew faint:
She knelt, so pure a thing, so free from mortal taint.

XXVI.

Anon his heart revives: her vespers done,
Of all its wreathèd pearls her hair she frees;
Unclasps her warmèd jewels one by one;
Loosens her fragrant bodice; by degrees
Her rich attire creeps rustling to her knees:
Half-hidden, like a mermaid in seaweed,
Pensive awhile she dreams awake, and sees,
In fancy, fair St. Agnes in her bed,
But dares not look behind, or all the charm is fled.

XXVII.

Soon, trembling in her soft and chilly nest,
In sort of wakeful swoon, perplexed she lay,
Until the poppied warmth of sleep oppressed
Her soothèd limbs, and soul fatigued away;

Flown, like a thought, until the morrow-day ;
Blissfully havened both from joy and pain ;
Clasped like a missal where swart Paynims pray ;
Blinded alike from sunshine and from rain,
As though a rose should shut, and be a bud again.

XXVIII.

Stolen to this paradise, and so entranced,
Porphyro gazed upon her empty dress,
And listened to her breathing, if it chanced
To wake into a slumberous tenderness ;
Which when he heard, that minute did he bless,
And breathed himself : then from the closet crept,
Noiseless as fear in a wide wilderness,
And over the hushed carpet, silent, stept,
And 'tween the curtains peeped, where, lo ! how fast she
    slept.

XXIX.

Then by the bedside, where the faded moon
Made a dim, silver twilight, soft he set
A table, and, half anguished, threw thereon
A cloth of woven crimson, gold, and jet :
O for some drowsy Morphean amulet !
The boisterous, midnight, festive clarion,
The kettledrum, and far-heard clarionet,
Affray his ears, though but in dying tone :
The hall-door shuts again, and all the noise is gone.

XXX.

And still she slept an azure-lidded sleep,
In blanchèd linen, smooth, and lavendered,
While he forth from the closet brought a heap
Of candied apple, quince, and plum, and gourd ;

With jellies soother than the creamy curd,
And lucent syrops, tinct with cinnamon ;
Manna and dates, in argosy transferred
From Fez ; and spicèd dainties, every one,
From silken Samarcand to cedared Lebanon.

XXXI.

These delicates he heaped with glowing hand
On golden dishes and in baskets bright
Of wreathèd silver : sumptuous they stand
In the retirèd quiet of the night,
Filling the chilly room with perfume light.
"And now, my love, my seraph fair awake !
Thou art my heaven, and I thy eremite :
Open thine eyes, for meek St. Agnes' sake,
Or I shall drowse beside thee, so my soul doth ache."

XXXII.

Thus whispering, his warm, unnervèd arm
Sank in her pillow. Shaded was her dream
By the dusk curtains :—'twas a midnight charm
Impossible to melt as icèd stream :
The lustrous salvers in the moonlight gleam ;
Broad golden fringe upon the carpet lies :
It seemed he never, never could redeem
From such a steadfast spell his lady's eyes ;
So mused awhile, entoiled in woofèd fantasies.

XXXIII.

Awakening up, he took her hollow lute—
Tumultuous,—and, in chords that tenderest be,
He played an ancient ditty, long since mute,
In Provence called, " La belle dame sans mercy " :

Close to her ear touching the melody ;
Wherewith disturbed, she uttered a soft moan :
He ceased—she panted quick—and suddenly
Her blue affrayèd eyes wide open shone :
Upon his knees he sank, pale as smooth-sculptured stone.

XXXIV.

Her eyes were open, but she still beheld,
Now wide awake, the vision of her sleep :
There was a painful change, that nigh expelled
The blisses of her dream so pure and deep
At which fair Madeline began to weep,
And moan forth witless words with many a sigh ;
While still her gaze on Porphyro would keep ;
Who knelt, with joinèd hands and piteous eye,
Fearing to move or speak, she looked so dreamingly.

XXXV.

"Ah, Porphyro ! " said she, " but even now
Thy voice was at sweet tremble in mine ear,
Made tuneable with every sweetest vow ;
And those sad eyes were spiritual and clear :
How changed thou art ! how pallid, chill, and drear !
Give me that voice again, my Porphyro,
Those looks immortal, those complaining dear !
Oh leave me not in this eternal woe,
For if thou diest, my love, I know not where to go ! "

XXXVI.

Beyond a mortal man impassioned far
At these voluptuous accents, he rose,
Ethereal, flushed, and like a throbbing star
Seen 'mid the sapphire heaven's deep repose ;

Into her dream he melted, as the rose
Blendeth its odour with the violet,—
Solution sweet : meantime the frost-wind blows
Like Love's alarum pattering the sharp sleet
Against the window-panes ; St. Agnes' moon hath set.

XXXVII.

'Tis dark : quick pattereth the flaw-blown sleet :
" This is no dream, my bride, my Madeline ! "
'Tis dark : the icèd gusts still rave and beat.
" No dream, alas ! alas ! and woe is mine !
Porphyro will leave me here to fade and pine.
Cruel ! what traitor could thee hither bring ?
I curse not, for my heart is lost in thine,
Though thou forsakest a deceivèd thing ;
A dove forlorn and lost with sick unprunèd wing."

XXXVIII.

" My Madeline ! sweet dreamer ! lovely bride !
Say, may I be for aye thy vassal blest ?
Thy beauty's shield, heart-shaped and vermeil dyed ?
Ah, silver shrine, here will I take my rest
After so many hours of toil and quest,
A famished pilgrim,—saved by miracle.
Though I have found, I will not rob thy nest
Saving of thy sweet self ; if thou think'st well
To trust, fair Madeline, to no rude infidel.

XXXIX.

" Hark ! 'tis an elfin-storm from fairy land,
Of haggard seeming, but a boon indeed :
Arise—arise ! the morning is at hand ;
The bloated wassaillers will never heed :

Let us away, my love, with happy speed;
There are no ears to hear, or eyes to see,—
Drowned all in Rhenish and the sleepy mead :
Awake ! arise ! my love, and fearless be,
For o'er the southern moors I have a home for thee."

XL.

She hurried at his words, beset with fears,
For there were sleeping dragons all around,
At glaring watch, perhaps, with ready spears—
Down the wide stairs a darkling way they found.
In all the house was heard no human sound.
A chain-drooped lamp was flickering by each door ;
The arras, rich with horseman, hawk, and hound,
Fluttered in the besieging wind's uproar ;
And the long carpets rose along the gusty floor.

XLI.

They glide, like phantoms, into the wide hall ;
Like phantoms, to the iron porch, they glide ;
Where lay the porter, in uneasy sprawl,
With a huge empty flagon by his side :
The wakeful bloodhound rose, and shook his hide,
But his sagacious eye an inmate owns :
By one, and one, the bolts full easy slide :
The chains lie silent on the footworn stones ;
The key turns, and the door upon its hinges groans.

XLII.

And they are gone : ay, ages long ago
These lovers fled away into the storm.
That night the Baron dreamt of many a woe,
And all his warrior-guests, with shade and form

Of witch, and demon, and large coffin-worm,
  Were long be-nightmared. Angela the old
Died palsy-twitched, with meagre face deform,
  The Beadsman, after thousand aves told,
For aye unsought-for slept amongst his ashes cold.

IX.—BYRON

MAZEPPA'S RIDE

IX.

' BRING forth the horse ! ' The horse was brought ;
  In truth, he was a noble steed,
  A Tartar of the Ukraine breed,
Who look'd as though the speed of thought
Were in his limbs ; but he was wild,
  Wild as the wild deer, and untaught,
With spur and bridle undefiled—
  'Twas but a day he had been caught ;
And snorting, with erected mane,
And struggling fiercely, but in vain,
In the full foam of wrath and dread
To me the desert-born was led :
They bound me on, that menial throng,
Upon his back with many a thong,
Then loosed him with a sudden lash—
Away !—away !—and on we dash !—
Torrents less rapid and less rash.

X.

"Away ! away ! my breath was gone,
I saw not where he hurried on :
'Twas scarcely yet the break of day,
And on he foam'd—away !—away !—
The last of human sounds which rose,
As I was darted from my foes,

Was the wild shout of savage laughter,
Which on the wind came roaring after
A moment from that rabble rout;
With sudden wrath I wrench'd my head,
  And snapp'd the cord which to the mane
  Had bound my neck in lieu of rein,
And, writhing half my form about,
Howl'd back my curse; but 'midst the tread,
The thunder of my courser's speed,
Perchance they did not hear nor heed:
It vexes me—for I would fain
Have paid their insult back again.
I paid it well in after days;
There is not of that castle-gate,
Its drawbridge and portcullis weight,
Stone, bar, moat, bridge, or barrier left;
Nor of its field a blade of grass,
  Save what grows on a ridge of wall,
  Where stood the hearthstone of the hall;
And many a time ye there might pass,
Nor dream that e'er that fortress was.
I saw its turrets in a blaze,
Their crackling battlements all cleft,
  And the hot lead pour down like rain
From off the scorch'd and blackening roof,
Whose thickness was not vengeance-proof.
  They little thought that day of pain,
When launch'd, as on the lightning's flash,
They bade me to destruction dash,
  That one day I should come again,
With twice five thousand horse, to thank
  The Count for his uncourteous ride.
They play'd me then a bitter prank,
  When, with the wild horse for my guide,
They bound me to his foaming flank.

At length I play'd them one as frank—
For time at last sets all things even—
  And if we do but watch the hour,
  There never yet was human power
Which could evade, if unforgiven
The patient search and vigil long
Of him who treasures up a wrong.

XI.

"Away, away, my steed and I,
  Upon the pinions of the wind,
  All human dwellings left behind ;
We sped like meteors through the sky,
When with its crackling sound the night
Is chequer'd with the northern light ;
Town—village—none were on our track,
  But a wild plain of far extent,
And bounded by a forest black ;
  And, save the scarce seen battlement
On distant heights of some strong hold,
Against the Tartars built of old,
No trace of man. The year before
A Turkish army had marched o'er ;
And where the Spahi's hoof hath trod,
The verdure flies the bloody sod ;—
The sky was dull, and dim, and grey,
  And a low breeze crept moaning by—
  I could have answered with a sigh—
But fast we fled, away, away,—
And I could neither sigh nor pray ;
And my cold sweat-drops fell like rain
Upon the courser's bristling mane ;
But, snorting still with rage and fear,
He flew upon his far career ;

At times I almost thought, indeed,
He must have slacken'd in his speed :
But no—my bound and slender frame
   Was nothing to his angry might
And merely like a spur became ;
Each motion which I made to free
My swoll'n limbs from their agony
   Increased his fury and affright ;
I tried my voice—'twas faint and low
But yet he swerv'd as from a blow ;
And, starting to each accent, sprang
As from a sudden trumpet's clang ;
Meantime my cords were wet with gore,
Which, oozing through my limbs, ran o'er ;
And in my tongue the thirst became
A something fierier than flame.

XII.

" We near'd the wild wood—'twas so wide
I saw no bounds on either side ;
'Twas studded with old sturdy trees,
That bent not to the roughest breeze
Which howls down from Siberia's waste
And strips the forest in its haste ;
But these were few and far between,
Set thick with shrubs more young and green,
Luxuriant with their annual leaves,
Ere strewn by those autumnal eves,
That nip the forest's foliage dead,
Discolour'd with a lifeless red,
Which stands thereon like stiffen'd gore
Upon the slain when battle's o'er,
And some long winter's night hath shed
Its frosts o'er every tombless head

So cold and stark the raven's beak
May peck unpierced each frozen cheek :
'Twas a wild waste of underwood,
And here and there a chestnut stood,
The strong oak, and the hardy pine ;
   But far apart—and well it were,
Or else a different lot were mine—
   The boughs gave way, and did not tear
My limbs ; and I found strength to bear
My wounds, already scarr'd with cold—
My bonds forbade to loose my hold.
We rustled through the leaves like wind,
Left shrubs, and trees, and wolves behind ;
By night I heard them on the track,
Their troop came hard upon our back,
With their long gallop, which can tire
The hound's deep hate and hunter's fire :
Where'er we flew they follow'd on,
Nor left us with the morning sun ;
Behind I saw them, scarce a rood,
At daybreak winding through the wood,
And through the night had heard their feet
Their stealing, rustling step repeat.
Oh ! how I wished for spear or sword,
At least to die amidst the horde,
And perish—if it must be so—
At bay, destroying many a foe.
When first my courser's race begun,
I wish'd the goal already won ;
But now I doubted strength and speed.
Vain doubt ! his swift and savage breed
Had nerved him like the mountain roe ;
Nor faster falls the blinding snow
Which whelms the peasant near the door
Whose threshold he shall cross no more.

Bewilder'd with the dazzling blast,
Than through the forest-paths he pass'd
Untired, untamed, and worse than wild ;
All furious as a favour'd child
Balk'd of its wish ; or fiercer still—
A woman piqued—who has her will.

XIII.

" The wood was pass'd ; 'twas more than noon,
But chill the air, although in June ;
Or it might be my veins ran cold—
Prolong'd endurance tames the bold ;
And I was then not what I seem,
But headlong as a wintry stream,
And wore my feelings out before
I well could count their causes o'er :
And what with fury, fear, and wrath,
The tortures which beset my path,
Cold, hunger, sorrow, shame, distress,
Thus bound in nature's nakedness ;
Sprung from a race whose rising blood,
When stirred beyond its calmer mood,
And trodden hard upon, is like
The rattlesnake's, in act to strike,
What marvel if this worn-out trunk
Beneath its woes a moment sunk ?
The earth gave way, the skies roll'd round.
I seem'd to sink upon the ground ;
But err'd, for I was fastly bound.
My heart turn'd sick, my brain grew sore,
And throbb'd awhile, then beat no more :
The skies spun like a mighty wheel ;
I saw the trees like drunkards reel,

And a slight flash sprang o'er my eyes,
Which saw no further : he who dies
Can die no more than then I died.
O'ertortured by that ghastly ride,
I felt the blackness come and go,
   And strove to wake ; but could not make
My senses climb up from below :
I felt as on a plank at sea,
When all the waves that dash o'er thee
At the same time upheave and whelm,
And hurl thee towards a desert realm.
My undulating life was as
The fancied lights that flitting pass
Our shut eyes in deep midnight, when
Fever begins upon the brain ;
But soon it pass'd, with little pain,
   But a confusion worse than such :
   I own that I should deem it much,
Dying, to feel the same again ;
And yet I do suppose we must
Feel far more ere we turn to dust :
No matter ; I have bared my brow
Full in Death's face—before—and now.

XIV.

" My thoughts came back ; where was I ? cold,
   And numb, and giddy : pulse by pulse
Life reassumed its lingering hold,
And throb by throb—till grown a pang
   Which for a moment could convulse,
   My blood reflow'd, though thick and chill ;
My ear with uncouth noises rang,
   My heart began once more to thrill ;

E

My sight return'd, though dim, alas !
And thicken'd, as it were, with glass.
Methought the dash of waves was nigh ;
There was a gleam, too, of the sky
Studded with stars ;—it is no dream ;
The wild horse swims the wilder stream !
The bright, broad river's gushing tide
Sweeps, winding onward, far and wide,
And we are half-way, struggling o'er
To yon unknown and silent shore.
The waters broke my hollow trance,
And with a temporary strength
    My stiffen'd limbs were rebaptized,
My courser's broad breast proudly braves,
And dashes off the ascending waves,
And onward we advance !
We reach the slippery shore at length,
    A haven I but little prized,
For all behind was dark and drear,
And all before was night and fear.
How many hours of night or day
In those suspended pangs I lay,
I could not tell ; I scarcely knew
If this were human breath I drew.

                          xv.

" With glossy skin, and dripping mane,
    And reeling limbs, and reeking flank,
The wild steed's sinewy nerves still strain
    Up the repelling bank.
We gain the top ; a boundless plain
Spreads through the shadow of the night,
    And onward, onward, onward, seems,
Like precipices in our dreams,

To stretch beyond the sight ;
And here and there a speck of white,
  Or scatter'd spot of dusky green,
In masses broke into the light,
As rose the moon upon my right :
  But nought distinctly seen
In the dim waste would indicate
The omen of a cottage gate ;
No twinkling taper from afar
Stood like a hospitable star ;
Not even an ignis-fatuus rose
To make him merry with my woes :
  That very cheat had cheer'd me then !
Although detected, welcome still,
Reminding me, through every ill
  Of the abodes of men.

XVI.

" Onward we went, but slack and slow ;
  His savage course at length o'erspent,
  The drooping courser, faint and low,
  Or feebly foaming went.
A sickly infant had had power
To guide him forward in that hour ;
  But useless all to me :
His new-born tameness nought avail'd—
My limbs were bound ; my force had fail'd,
  Perchance, had they been free.
With feeble effort still I tried
To rend the bonds so starkly tied,
  But still it was in vain ;
  My limbs were only wrung the more,
And soon the idle strife gave o'er,
  Which but prolong'd their pain ;

The dizzy race seem'd almost done,
Although no goal was nearly won ;
Some streaks announced the coming sun—
    How slow, alas, he came !
Methought that mist of dawning grey
Would never dapple into day ;
How heavily it roll'd away—
    Before the eastern flame
Rose crimson, and deposed the stars,
And call'd the radiance from their cars,
And fill'd the earth, from his deep throne,
With lonely lustre, all his own.

XVII.

" Up rose the sun : the mists were curl'd
Back from the solitary world
Which lay around, behind, before :
What booted it to traverse o'er
Plain, forest, river ? Man nor brute,
Nor dint of hoof, nor print of foot,
Lay in the wild, luxuriant soil ;
No sign of travel—none of toil ;
The very air was mute ;
And not an insect's shrill small horn,
No matin bird's new voice, was borne
From herb nor thicket. Many a werst,
Panting as if his heart would burst,
The weary brute still stagger'd on ;
And still we were—or seem'd—alone.
At length, while reeling on our way,
Methought I heard a courser neigh,
From out yon tuft of blackening firs.
Is it the wind those branches stirs ?

No, no ! from out the forest prance
  A trampling troop ; I see them come !
In one vast squadron they advance !
  I strove to cry—my lips were dumb.
The steeds rush on in plunging pride ;
But where are they the reins to guide ?
A thousand horse—and none to ride !
With flowing tail, and flying mane,
Wide nostrils, never stretch'd by pain,
Mouths bloodless to the bit or rein,
And feet that iron never shod,
And flanks unscarr'd by spur or rod,
A thousand horse, the wild, the free,
Like waves that follow o'er the sea,
  Came thickly thundering on,
As if our faint approach to meet ;
The sight re-nerved my courser's feet,
A moment staggering, feebly fleet,
A moment, with a faint low neigh,
  He answered, and then fell.
With gasps and glazing eyes he lay,
And reeking limbs immoveable,
    His first and last career is done !
On came the troop—they saw him stoop,
  They saw me strangely bound along
  His back with many a bloody thong :
They stop—they start—they snuff the air,
Gallop a moment here and there,
Approach, retire, wheel round and round,
Then plunging back with sudden bound,
Headed by one black mighty steed,
Who seem'd the patriarch of his breed,
  Without a single speck or hair
Of white upon his shaggy hide :
They snort, they foam, neigh, swerve aside,

And backward to the forest fly,
By instinct, from a human eye.
　　They left me there, to my dispair,
Link'd to the dead and stiffening wretch,
Whose lifeless limbs beneath me stretch,
Relieved from that unwonted weight,
From whence I could not extricate
Nor him, nor me ;—and there we lay,
　　The dying on the dead !
I little deem'd another day
　　Would see my houseless, helpless head.

"And there from morn till twilight bound,
I felt the heavy hours toil round,
With just enough of life to see
My last of suns go down on me,
In hopeless certainty of mind,
That makes us feel at length resign'd
To that which our foreboding years
Present the worst and last of fears
Inevitable—even a boon,
Nor more unkind for coming soon ;
Yet shunn'd and dreaded with such care,
As if it only were a snare
　　That prudence might escape :
At times both wish'd for and implored,
At times sought with self-pointed sword,
Yet still a dark and hideous close
To even intolerable woes,
　　And welcome in no shape.
And, strange to say, the sons of pleasure,
They who have revell'd beyond measure
In beauty, wassail, wine, and treasure.
Die calm, or calmer, oft than he
Whose heritage was misery :

For he who hath in turn run through
All that was beautiful and new,
   Hath nought to hope, and nought to leave :
And, save the future (which is view'd
Not quite as men are base or good,
But as their nerves may be endued),
   With nought perhaps to grieve :
The wretch still hopes his woes must end,
And Death, whom he should deem his friend,
Appears to his distemper'd eyes,
Arrived to rob him of his prize,
The tree of his new Paradise.
To-morrow would have given him all,
Repaid his pangs, repair'd his fall :
To-morrow would have been the first
Of days no more deplored or curst,
But bright, and long, and beckoning years,
Seen dazzling through the mist of tears,
Guerdon of many a painful hour ;
To-morrow would have given him power
To rule, to shine, to smite, to save—
And must it dawn upon his grave ?

XVIII.

" The sun was sinking—still I lay
   Chain'd to the chill and stiffening steed ;
I thought to mingle there our clay,
   And my dim eyes of death had need,
   No hope arose of being freed :
I cast my last looks up the sky,
   And there between me and the sun
I saw the expecting raven fly,
Who scarce would wait till both should die,
   Ere his repast begun.

He flew, and perch'd, then flew once more,
And each time nearer than before ;
I saw his wing through twilight flit,
And once so near me he alit,
 I could have smote, but lack'd the strength ;
But the slight motion of my hand,
And feeble scratching of the sand,
The exerted throat's faint struggling noise,
Which scarcely could be call'd a voice,
 Together scared him off at length.—
I know no more—my latest dream
 Is something of a lovely star
 Which fix'd my dull eyes from afar,
And went and came with wandering beam,
And of the cold, dull, swimming, dense
Sensation of recurring sense,
And then subsiding back to death,
And then again a little breath,
A little thrill, a short suspense,
An icy sickness curdling o'er
My heart, and sparks that cross'd my brain—
A gasp, a throb, a start of pain,
A sigh, and nothing more.

XIX.

" I woke—Where was I ?—Do I see
A human face look down on me ?
And doth a roof above me close ?
Do these limbs on a couch repose ?
Is this a chamber where I lie ?
And is it mortal, yon bright eye,
That watches me with gentle glance ?
 I close my own again once more,
As doubtful that the former trance
 Could not as yet be o'er.

A slender girl, long-hair'd and tall,
Sate watching by the cottage wall ;
The sparkle of her eye I caught,
Even with my first return of thought ;
For ever and anon she threw
 A prying, pitying glance on me
 With her black eyes so wild and free :
I gazed, and gazed, until I knew
 No vision it could be,—
But that I lived, and was released
From adding to the vulture's feast :
And when the Cossack maid beheld
My heavy eyes at length unseal'd,
She smiled, and I essay'd to speak,
 But fail'd—and she approach'd and made
 With lip and finger signs that said,
I must not strive as yet to break
The silence, till my strength should be
Enough to leave my accents free ;
And then her hand on mine she laid,
And smooth'd the pillow for my head,
And stole along on tiptoe tread,
 And gently oped the door, and spake
In whispers—ne'er was voice so sweet !
Even music follow'd her light feet ;—
 But those she call'd were not awake.
And she went forth ; but, ere she pass'd,
Another look on me she cast,
 Another sign she made, to say
That I had nought to fear, that all
Were near, at my command or call,
 And she would not delay
Her due return :—while she was gone,
Methought I felt too much alone.

E*

xx.

"She came with mother and with sire—
What need of more !—I will not tire
With long recital of the rest
Since I became the Cossack's guest.
They found me senseless on the plain—
   They bore me to the nearest hut—
They brought me into life again—
Me—one day o'er their realm to reign !
   Thus the vain fool who strove to glut
His rage, refining on my pain,
   Sent me forth to the wilderness,
Bound, naked, bleeding, and alone,
To pass the desert to a throne,—
   What mortal his own doom may guess ?
   Let none despond, let none despair !
To-morrow the Borysthenes
May see our coursers graze at ease
Upon his Turkish bank ; and never
Had I such welcome for a river
   As I shall yield when safely there.
Comrades, good night ! "—The Hetman threw
   His length beneath the oak-tree shade,
   With leafy couch already made,
A bed nor comfortless nor new
To him who took his rest whene'er
The hour arrived, no matter where :
   His eyes the hastening slumbers steep.
And if ye marvel Charles forgot
To thank his tale, *he* wondered not—
   The king had been an hour asleep.

X.—BROWNING

PHEIDIPPIDES

Χαίρετε, νικῶμεν.

FIRST I salute this soil of the blessed, river and rock !
Gods of my birthplace, dæmons and heroes, honour to all !
Then I name thee, claim thee for our patron, co-equal in
    praise
—Ay, with Zeus the Defender, with Her of the ægis and spear
Also, ye of the bow and the buskin, praised be your peer,
Now, henceforth and for ever,—O latest to whom I upraise
Hand and heart and voice ! For Athens, leave pasture and
    flock !
Present to help, potent to save, Pan—patron I call !

Archons of Athens, topped by the tettix, see, I return !
See, 'tis myself here standing alive, no spectre that speaks ! 10
Crowned with the myrtle, did you command me, Athens and
    you,
" Run, Pheidippides, run and race, reach Sparta for aid !
Persia has come, we are here, where is She ? " Your command
    I obeyed,
Ran and raced : like stubble, some field which a fire runs
    through,
Was the space between city and city : two days, two nights
    did I burn
Over the hills, under the dales, down pits and up peaks.

Into their midst I broke : breath served but for " Persia has
    come !
Persia bids Athens proffer slaves'-tribute, water and earth ;

Razed to the ground is Eretria—but Athens, shall Athens sink,

Drop into dust and die—the flower of Hellas utterly die,   20

Die, with the wide world spitting at Sparta, the stupid, the stander-by ?

Answer me quick, what help, what hand do you stretch o'er destruction's brink ?

How,—when ? No care for my limbs !—there's lightning in all and some—

Fresh and fit your message to bear, once lips give it birth ! "

O my Athens—Sparta love thee ? Did Sparta respond ?

Every face of her leered in a furrow of envy, mistrust,

Malice,—each eye of her gave me its glitter of gratified hate !

Gravely they turned to take counsel, to cast for excuses. I stood

Quivering,—the limbs of me fretting as fire frets, an inch from dry wood :

" Persia has come, Athens asks aid, and still they debate ? 30

Thunder, thou Zeus ! Athene, are Spartans a quarry beyond

Swing of thy spear ? Phoibos and Artemis, clang them ' Ye must ' ! "

No bolt launched from Olumpos ! Lo, their answer at last !

" Has Persia come,—does Athens ask aid,—may Sparta befriend ?

Nowise precipitate judgment—too weighty the issue at stake !

Count we no time lost time which lags through respect to the Gods !

Ponder that precept of old, ' No warfare, whatever the odds

In your favour, so long as the moon, half-orbed, is unable to take

Full circle her state in the sky ! ' Already she rounds to it fast :

Athens must wait, patient as we—who judgment suspend." 40

Athens,—except for that sparkle,—thy name, I had mould-
ered to ash !
That sent a blaze through my blood ; off, off and away was
I back,
—Not one word to waste, one look to lose on the false and
the vile !
Yet " O Gods of my land ! " I cried, as each hillock and plain,
Wood and stream, I knew, I named, rushing past them again,
" Have ye kept faith, proved mindful of honours we paid you
erewhile ?
Vain was the filleted victim, the fulsome libation ! Too rash
Love in its choice, paid you so largely service so slack !

" Oak and olive and bay,—I bid you cease to enwreathe
Brows made bold by your leaf ! Fade at the Persian's foot, 50
You that, our patrons were pledged, should never adorn a
slave !
Rather I hail thee, Parnes,—trust to thy wild waste tract !
Treeless, herbless, lifeless mountain ! What matter if slacked
My speed may hardly be, for homage to crag and to cave
No deity deigns to drape with verdure ? at least I can breathe,
Fear in thee no fraud from the blind, no lie from the mute ! "

Such my cry as, rapid, I ran over Parnes' ridge ;
Gully and gap I clambered and cleared till, sudden, a bar
Jutted, a stoppage of stone against me, blocking the way. 59
Right ! for I minded the hollow to traverse, the fissure
across :
" Where I could enter, there I depart by ! Night in the fosse ?
Athens to aid ? Though the dive were through Erebos, thus
I obey,—

Out of the day dive, into the day as bravely arise ! No bridge
Better ! "—when—ha ! what was it I came on, of wonders
    that are ?

There, in the cool of a cleft, sat he—majestical Pan !
Ivy drooped wanton, kissed his head, moss cushioned his
    hoof :
All the great God was good in the eyes grave-kindly—the
    curl
Carved on the bearded cheek, amused at a mortal's awe,
As, under the human trunk, the goat-thighs grand I saw.
" Halt, Pheidippides ! "—halt I did, my brain of a whirl :   70
" Hither to me ! Why pale in my presence ? " he gracious
    began :
" How is it,—Athens, only in Hellas, holds me aloof ?

"Athens, she only, rears me no fane, makes me no feast !
Wherefore ? Than I what godship to Athens more helpful of
    old ?
Ay, and still, and for ever her friend ! Test Pan, trust me !
Go, bid Athens take heart, laugh Persia to scorn, have faith
In the temples and the tombs ! Go, say to Athens, ' The Goat-
    God saith :
When Persia—so much as strews not the soil—is cast in the
    sea,
Then praise Pan who fought in the ranks with your most and
    least,
Goat-thigh to greaved-thigh, made one cause with the free
    and the bold ! '

" Say Pan saith : ' Let this, foreshowing the place, be the
    pledge ! ' "
(Gay, the liberal hand held out this herbage I bear   82
—Fennel—I grasped it a-tremble with dew—whatever it
    bode)

" While, as for thee . . ." But enough ! He was gone. If
    I ran hitherto—
Be sure that, the rest of my journey, I ran no longer, but
    flew.
Parnes to Athens—earth no more, the air was my road :
Here am I back. Praise Pan, we stand no more on the razor's
    edge !
Pan for Athens, Pan for me ! I too have a guerdon rare !

Then spoke Miltiades. "And thee, best runner of Greece,   89
Whose limbs did duty indeed,—what gift is promised thy-
    self ?
Tell it us straightway,—Athens the mother demands of her
    son ! "
Rosily blushed the youth : he paused : but, lifting at length
His eyes from the ground, it seemed as he gathered the rest
    of his strength
Into the utterance—" Pan spoke thus : 'For what thou hast
    done
Count on a worthy reward ! Henceforth be allowed thee
    release
From the racer's toil, no vulgar reward in praise or in pelf ! '

" I am bold to believe, Pan means reward the most to my
    mind !
Fight I shall, with our foremost, wherever this fennel may
    grow,—
Pound—Pan helping us—Persia to dust, and, under the deep,
Whelm her away for ever ; and then,—no Athens to
    save,—
Marry a certain maid, I know keeps faith to the brave,—   101
Hie to my house and home : and when my children shall creep
Close to my knees,—recount how the God was awful yet kind,
Promised their sire reward to the full—rewarding him—so ! "

Unforeseeing one ! Yes, he fought on the Marathon day :
So, when Persia was dust, all cried, " To Akropolis !
Run, Pheidippides, one race more ! the meed is thy due !
'Athens is saved, thank Pan,' go shout ! " He flung down his
    shield,
Ran like fire once more : and the space 'twixt the Fennel-
    field
And Athens was stubble again, a field which a fire runs
    through,
Till in he broke : " Rejoice, we conquer ! " Like wine
    through clay,
Joy in his blood bursting his heart, he died—the bliss !   112

So, to this day, when friend meets friend, the word of salute
Is still " Rejoice ! "—his word which brought rejoicing
    indeed.

So is Pheidippides happy for ever,—the noble strong man
Who could race like a God, bear the face of a God, whom a
    God loved so well ;
He saw the land saved he had helped to save, and was suffered
    to tell
Such tidings, yet never decline, but, gloriously as he began,
So to end gloriously—once to shout, thereafter be mute :   119
"Athens is saved ! "—Pheidippides dies in the shout for his
    meed.

(*Reprinted by permission of Mr. John Murray.*)

XI.—COLERIDGE

THE RIME OF THE ANCIENT MARINER

Part I.

It is an ancient Mariner,
And he stoppeth one of three.
" By thy long grey beard and glittering eye,
Now wherefore stopp'st thou me ?

An ancient Mariner meeteth three gallants bidden to a wedding-feast, and detaineth one.

The Bridegroom's doors are open'd wide,
And I am next of kin ;
The guests are met, the feast is set :
May'st hear the merry din."

He holds him with his skinny hand,
" There was a ship," quoth he.   10
" Hold off ! unhand me, grey-beard loon ! "
Eftsoons his hand dropt he.

He holds him with his glittering eye—
The Wedding-Guest stood still,
And listens like a three years' child :
The Mariner hath his will.

The Wedding-Guest is spell-bound by the eye of the old seafaring man, and constrained to hear his tale

The Wedding-Guest sat on a stone :
He cannot choose but hear ;
And thus spake on that ancient man,
The bright-eyed Mariner :   20

" The ship was cheer'd, the harbour clear'd,
Merrily did we drop
Below the kirk, below the hill,
Below the lighthouse top.

The Mariner
tells how the
ship sailed
southward with
a good wind
and fair
weather, till
it reached the
Line.

The Sun came up upon the left,
Out of the sea came he !
And he shone bright, and on the right
Went down into the sea.

Higher and higher every day,
Till over the mast at noon——"   30
The Wedding-Guest here beat his breast,
For he heard the loud bassoon.

The Wedding-
Guest heareth
the bridal
music ; but the
Mariner con-
tinueth his tale.

The bride hath paced into the hall,
Red as a rose is she ;
Nodding their heads before her goes
The merry minstrelsy.

The Wedding-Guest he beat his breast,
Yet he cannot choose but hear ;
And thus spake on that ancient man,
The bright-eyed Mariner :   40

The ship drawn
by a storm to-
ward the South
Pole.

"And now the Storm-blast came, and he
Was tyrannous and strong :
He struck with his o'ertaking wings,
And chased us south along.

With sloping masts and dipping prow,
As who pursued with yell and blow
Still treads the shadow of his foe,
And forward bends his head,
The ship drove fast, loud roar'd the blast,
And southward aye we fled.   50

And now there came both mist and snow
And it grew wondrous cold :
And ice, mast-high, came floating by,
As green as emerald.

And through the drifts the snowy clifts
Did send a dismal sheen :
Nor shapes of men nor beasts we ken—
The ice was all between.

The land of ice
and of fearful
sounds, where
no living thing
was to be seen.

The ice was here, the ice was there,
The ice was all around :   60
It crack'd and growl'd, and roar'd and howl'd,
Like noises in a swound !

At length did cross an Albatross,
Thorough the fog it came ;
As if it had been a Christian soul,
We hail'd it in God's name.

Till a great
sea-bird, called
the Albatross,
came through
the snow-fog,
and was re-
ceived with
great joy and
hospitality.

It ate the food it ne'er had eat,
And round and round it flew.
The ice did split with a thunder-fit ;
The helmsman steer'd us through !   70

A good south wind sprung up behind ;
The Albatross did follow,
And every day, for food or play,
Came to the mariners' hollo !

And lo ! the
Albatross
proveth a bird
of good omen,
and followeth
the ship as it
returned north-
ward through
fog and floating
ice.

In mist or cloud, on mast or shroud,
It perch'd for vespers nine ;
Whiles all the night, through fog-smoke white,
Glimmer'd the white moonshine."

The ancient
Mariner in-
hospitably
killeth the pious
bird of good
omen.

" God save thee, ancient Mariner,
From the fiends, that plague thee thus !—   80
Why look'st thou so ? "—" With my crossbow
I shot the Albatross."

PART II.

" The Sun now rose upon the right :
Out of the sea came he,
Still hid in mist, and on the left
Went down into the sea.

And the good south wind still blew behind,
But no sweet bird did follow,
Nor any day for food or play
Came to the mariners' hollo !   90

His shipmates
cry out against
the ancient
Mariner for
killing the bird
of good luck.

And I had done a hellish thing,
And it would work 'em woe :
For all averr'd I had kill'd the bird
That made the breeze to blow.
Ah, wretch ! said they, the bird to slay
That made the breeze to blow !

But when the
fog cleared off,
they justify the
same, and thus
make them-
selves accom-
plices in the
crime.

Nor dim nor red, like God's own head,
The glorious sun uprist :
Then all averr'd I had kill'd the bird
That brought the fog and mist.   100
'Twas right, said they, such birds to slay,
That bring the fog and mist.

The fair breeze
continues ; the
ship enters the
Pacific Ocean,
and sails north-
ward, even till
it reaches the
Line.

The fair breeze blew, the white foam flew,
The furrow follow'd free ;
We were the first that ever burst
Into that silent sea.

Down dropt the breeze, the sails dropt down,
'Twas sad as sad could be ;
And we did speak only to break
The silence of the sea !

The ship hath been suddenly becalmed.

110

All in a hot and copper sky,
The bloody Sun, at noon,
Right up above the mast did stand,
No bigger than the Moon.

Day after day, day after day,
We stuck, nor breath nor motion ;
As idle as a painted ship
Upon a painted ocean.

Water, water, everywhere,
And all the boards did shrink ;
Water, water, everywhere,
Nor any drop to drink.

And the Albatross begins to be avenged.

120

The very deep did rot : O Christ !
That ever this should be !
Yea, slimy things did crawl with legs
Upon the slimy sea.

About, about, in reel and rout
The death-fires danced at night ;
The water, like a witch's oils,
Burnt green, and blue, and white.

130

And some in dreams assurèd were
Of the Spirit that plagued us so ;
Nine fathom deep he had follow'd us
From the land of mist and snow.

A Spirit had followed them; one of the invisible inhabitants of this planet, neither departed souls nor angels ; concerning whom the learned Jew, Josephus, and the Platonic Constantinopolitan, Michael Psellus, may be consulted. They are very numerous, and there is no climate or element, without one or more.

And every tongue, through utter drought,
Was wither'd at the root ;
We could not speak, no more than if
We had been choked with soot.

The shipmates, in their sore distress, would fain throw the whole guilt on the ancient Mariner : in sign whereof they hang the dead sea-bird round his neck.

Ah ! well-a-day ! what evil looks
Had I from old and young !   140
Instead of the cross, the Albatross
About my neck was hung.

PART III.

" There passed a weary time. Each throat
Was parch'd, and glazed each eye.
A weary time ! a weary time !
How glazed each weary eye !
When looking westward, I beheld
A something in the sky.

The ancient Mariner be-holdeth a sign in the element afar off.

At first it seem'd a little speck,
And then it seem'd a mist ;   150
It moved and moved, and took at last
A certain shape, I wist.

A speck, a mist, a shape, I wist !
And still it near'd and near'd :
As if it dodged a water-sprite,
It plunged, and tack'd, and veer'd.

At its nearer approach, it seemeth him to be a ship ; and at a dear ransom he freeth his speech from the bonds of thirst.

With throats unslaked, with black lips baked,
We could nor laugh nor wail :
Through utter drought all dumb we stood !
I bit my arm, I suck'd the blood,   160
And cried, 'A sail ! a sail ! '

With throats unslaked, with black lips baked,
Agape they heard me call :
Gramercy ! they for joy did grin,
And all at once their breath drew in,
As they were drinking all.

A flash of joy;

See ! see ! (I cried) she tacks no more !
Hither to work us weal—
Without a breeze, without a tide,
She steadies with upright keel !

And horror follows. For can it be a ship that comes onward without wind or tide ?

170

The western wave was all aflame,
The day was wellnigh done !
Almost upon the western wave
Rested the broad, bright Sun ;
When that strange shape drove suddenly
Betwixt us and the Sun.

And straight the Sun was fleck'd with bars
(Heaven's Mother send us grace !),
As if through a dungeon-grate he peer'd
With broad and burning face.

It seemeth him but the skeleton of a ship.

180

Alas ! (thought I, and my heart beat loud)
How fast she nears and nears !
Are those her sails that glance in the Sun,
Like restless gossameres ?

Are those her ribs through which the Sun
Did peer, as through a grate ?
And is that Woman all her crew ?
Is that a Death ? and are there two ?
Is Death that Woman's mate ?

And its ribs are seen as bars on the face of the setting Sun. The Spectre-Woman and her Death-mate, and no other, on board the skeleton ship. Like vessel, like crew!

Her lips were red, her looks were free,   190
Her locks were yellow as gold :
Her skin was as white as leprosy,
The Nightmare Life-in-Death was she,
Who thicks man's blood with cold.

Death and Life-in-Death have diced for the ship's crew, and she (the latter) winneth the ancient Mariner.

The naked hulk alongside came,
And the twain were casting dice ;
' The game is done ! I've won ! I've won ! '
Quoth she, and whistles thrice.

No twilight within the courts of the Sun.

The Sun's rim dips ; the stars rush out :
At one stride comes the dark ;   200
With far-heard whisper, o'er the sea,
Off shot the spectre-bark.

We listen'd and look'd sideways up !
Fear at my heart, as at a cup,
My life-blood seem'd to sip !
The stars were dim, and thick the night,
The steersman's face by his lamp gleam'd white ;
From the sails the dew did drip—

At the rising of the Moon,

Till clomb above the eastern bar
The hornèd Moon, with one bright star   210
Within the nether tip.

One after another,

One after one, by the star-dogg'd Moon,
Too quick for groan or sigh,
Each turn'd his face with a ghastly pang,
And cursed me with his eye.

His shipmates drop down dead.

Four times fifty living men
(And I heard nor sigh nor groan),
With heavy thump, a lifeless lump,
They dropp'd down one by one.

The souls did from their bodies fly—   220
They fled to bliss or woe !
And every soul, it pass'd me by
Like the whizz of my crossbow ! "

But Life-in-Death begins her work on the ancient Mariner.

Part IV.

" I fear thee, ancient Mariner !
I fear thy skinny hand !
And thou art long, and lank, and brown,
As is the ribb'd sea-sand.

The Wedding-Guest feareth that a spirit is talking to him.

I fear thee and thy glittering eye,
And thy skinny hand so brown."—
" Fear not, fear not, thou Wedding-Guest !   230
This body dropt not down.

But the ancient Mariner assureth him of his bodily life, and proceedeth to relate his horrible penance.

Alone, alone, all, all alone,
Alone on a wide, wide sea !
And never a saint took pity on
My soul in agony.

The many men, so beautiful !
And they all dead did lie :
And a thousand thousand slimy things
Lived on ; and so did I.

He despiseth the creatures of the calm.

I look'd upon the rotting sea,   240
And drew my eyes away ;
I look'd upon the rotting deck,
And there the dead men lay.

And envieth that they should live, and so many lie dead.

I look'd to heaven, and tried to **pray** ;
But or ever a prayer had gusht,
A wicked whisper came, and made
My heart as dry as dust.

I closed my lids, and kept them close,
And the balls like pulses beat ;   249
For the sky and the sea, and the sea and the sky,
Lay like a load on my weary eye,
And the dead were at my feet.

*But the curse
liveth for him
in the eyes of the
dead men.*

The cold sweat melted from their limbs,
Nor rot nor reek did they :
The look with which they look'd on me
Had never pass'd away.

An orphan's curse would drag to hell
A spirit from on high ;
But oh ! more horrible than that
Is the curse in a dead man's eye !   260
Seven days, seven nights, I saw that curse,
And yet I could not die.

*In his loneliness
and fixedness
he yearneth
towards the
journeying
Moon, and the
stars that still
sojourn, yet still*

The moving Moon went up the sky,
And nowhere did abide ;
Softly she was going up,
And a star or two beside—

*move onward ; and everywhere the blue sky belongs to them, and is their appointed rest
and their native country and their own natural homes, which they enter unannounced,
as lords that are certainly expected, and yet there is a silent joy at their arrival.*

Her beams bemock'd the sultry main,
Like April hoar-frost spread ;
But where the ship's huge shadow lay,
The charmèd water burnt alway
A still and awful red.   270

*By the light of
the Moon he
beholdeth God's
creatures of the
great calm.*

Beyond the shadow of the ship,
I watch'd the water-snakes :
They moved in tracks of shining white,
And when they rear'd, the elfish light
Fell off in hoary flakes.

Within the shadow of the ship
I watch'd their rich attire :
Blue, glossy green, and velvet black,
They coil'd and swam ; and every track   280
Was a flash of golden fire.

O happy living things ! no tongue
Their beauty might declare :
A spring of love gush'd from my heart,
And I bless'd them unaware :
Sure my kind saint took pity on me,
And I bless'd them unaware.

Their beauty and their happiness.

He blesseth them in his heart.

The selfsame moment I could pray ;
And from my neck so free
The Albatross fell off, and sank   290
Like lead into the sea.

The spell begins to break.

PART V.

" O sleep ! it is a gentle thing,
Beloved from pole to pole !
To Mary Queen the praise be given !
She sent the gentle sleep from Heaven,
That slid into my soul.

The silly buckets on the deck,
That had so long remain'd,
I dreamt that they were fill'd with dew ;
And when I awoke, it rain'd.   300

By grace of the holy Mother, the ancient Mariner is refreshed with rain.

My lips were wet, my throat was cold,
My garments all were dank ;
Sure I had drunken in my dreams,
And still my body drank.

I moved, and could not feel my limbs :
I was so light—almost
I thought that I had died in sleep,
And was a blessèd ghost.

He heareth
sounds and
seeth strange
sights and
commotions
in the sky and
the element.

And soon I heard a roaring wind :
It did not come anear ;   310
But with its sound it shook the sails,
That were so thin and sere.

The upper air burst into life ;
And a hundred fire-flags sheen ;
To and fro they were hurried about !
And to and fro, and in and out,
The wan stars danced between.

And the coming wind did roar more loud,
And the sails did sigh like sedge ;   319
And the rain pour'd down from one black cloud;
The Moon was at its edge.

The thick black cloud was cleft, and still
The Moon was at its side ;
Like waters shot from some high crag,
The lightning fell with never a jag,
A river steep and wide.

The bodies of
the ship's crew
are inspired,
and the ship
moves on ;

The loud wind never reach'd the ship,
Yet now the ship moved on !
Beneath the lightning and the Moon
The dead men gave a groan.   330

They groan'd, they stirr'd, they all uprose,
Nor spake, nor moved their eyes ;
It had been strange, even in a dream,
To have seen those dead men rise.

The helmsman steer'd, the ship moved on ;
Yet never a breeze up-blew ;
The mariners all 'gan work the ropes,
Where they were wont to do ;
They raised their limbs like lifeless tools—
We were a ghastly crew.   340

The body of my brother's son
Stood by me, knee to knee :
The body and I pull'd at one rope,
But he said naught to me."

" I fear thee, ancient Mariner ! "
" Be calm, thou Wedding-Guest :
'Twas not those souls that fled in pain,
Which to their corses came again,
But a troop of spirits blest :

But not by the souls of the men, nor by demons of earth or middle air, but by a blessed troop of angelic spirits, sent down by the invocation of the guardian saint.

For when it dawn'd—they dropp'd their arms,
And cluster'd round the mast ;   351
Sweet sounds rose slowly through their mouths,
And from their bodies pass'd.

Around, around, flew each sweet sound,
Then darted to the Sun ;
Slowly the sounds came back again,
Now mix'd, now one by one.

Sometimes a-dropping from the sky
I heard the skylark sing ;
Sometimes all little birds that are,   360
How they seem'd to fill the sea and air
With their sweet jargoning !

And now 'twas like all instruments,
Now like a lonely flute ;
And now it is an angel's song,
That makes the Heavens be mute.

It ceased ; yet still the sails made on
A pleasant noise till noon,
A noise like of a hidden brook
In the leafy month of June,   370
That to the sleeping woods all night
Singeth a quiet tune.

Till noon we quietly sail'd on,
Yet never a breeze did breathe :
Slowly and smoothly went the ship,
Moved onward from beneath.

The lonesome
Spirit from the
South Pole
carries on the
ship as far as
the Line, in
obedience to the
angelic troop,
but still re-
quireth ven-
geance.

Under the keel nine fathom deep,
From the land of mist and snow,
The Spirit slid : and it was he
That made the ship to go.   380
The sails at noon left off their tune,
And the ship stood still also.

The Sun, right up above the mast,
Had fix'd her to the ocean :
But in a minute she 'gan stir,
With a short uneasy motion—
Backwards and forwards half her length
With a short uneasy motion.

Then like a pawing horse let go,
She made a sudden bound :   390
It flung the blood into my head,
And I fell down in a swound.

How long in that same fit I lay,
I have not to declare ;
But ere my living life return'd,
I heard, and in my soul discern'd
Two voices in the air.

' Is it he ? ' quoth one, ' is this the man ?
By Him who died on cross,
With his cruel bow he laid full low   400
The harmless Albatross.

The Spirit who bideth by himself
In the land of mist and snow,
He loved the bird that loved the man
Who shot him with his bow.'

The other was a softer voice,
As soft as honey-dew :
Quoth he, ' The man hath penance done,
And penance more will do.'

The Polar Spirit's fellow-demons, the invisible inhabitants of the element, take part in his wrong ; and two of them relate, one to the other, that penance long and heavy for the ancient Mariner hath been accorded to the Polar Spirit, who returneth southward.

Part VI.

First Voice :

" ' But tell me, tell me ! speak again,   410
Thy soft response renewing—
What makes that ship drive on so fast ?
What is the Ocean doing ? "

Second Voice :

' Still as a slave before his lord,
The Ocean hath no blast ;
His great bright eye most silently
Up to the Moon is cast—

If he may know which way to go;
For she guides him smooth or grim.
See, brother, see! how graciously   420
She looketh down on him.'

First Voice:

'But why drives on that ship so fast,
Without a wave or wind?'

The Marinei
hath been cast
into a trance;
for the angelic
power causeth
the vessel to
drive northward
faster than
human life
could endure.

Second Voice:

'The air is cut away before,
And closes from behind.

Fly, brother, fly! more high, more high!
Or we shall be belated:
For slow and slow that ship will go,
When the Mariner's trance is abated.'

The super-
natural motion
is retarded;
the Mariner
wakes, and
his penance
begins anew

I woke, and we were sailing on   430
As in a gentle weather:
'Twas night, calm night, the Moon was high;
The dead men stood together.

All stood together on the deck,
For a charnel-dungeon fitter:
All fix'd on me their stony eyes,
That in the Moon did glitter.

The pang, the curse, with which they died,
Had never pass'd away:
I could not draw my eyes from theirs,   440
Nor turn them up to pray.

And now this spell was snapt : once more
I viewed the ocean green,
And look'd far forth, yet little saw
Of what had else been seen—

The curse is finally expiated.

Like one that on a lonesome road
Doth walk in fear and dread,
And having once turn'd round, walks on
And turns no more his head ;
Because he knows a frightful fiend   450
Doth close behind him tread.

But soon there breathed a wind on me,
Nor sound nor motion made :
Its path was not upon the sea,
In ripple or in shade.

It raised my hair, it fann'd my cheek
Like a meadow-gale of spring—
It mingled strangely with my fears,
Yet felt like a welcoming.

Swiftly, swiftly flew the ship,   460
Yet she sailed softly too :
Sweetly, sweetly blew the breeze—
On me alone it blew.

O dream of joy ! is this indeed
The lighthouse top I see ?
Is this the hill ? is this the kirk ?
Is this mine own countree ?

And the ancient Mariner be-holdeth his native country.

We drifted o'er the harbour bar,
And I with sobs did pray—
O let me be awake, my God !   470
Or let me sleep alway.

F

The harbour-bay was clear as glass,
So smoothly it was strewn !
And on the bay the moonlight lay,
And the shadow of the Moon.

The rock shone bright, the kirk no less
That stands above the rock :
The moonlight steep'd in silentness
The steady weathercock.

The angelic
spirits leave the
dead bodies.

And the bay was white with silent light,   480
Till rising from the same,
Full many shapes, that shadows were,
In crimson colours came.

And appear in
their own forms
of light.

A little distance from the prow
Those crimson shadows were :
I turn'd my eyes upon the deck—
O Christ ! what saw I there !

Each corse lay flat, lifeless and flat,
And, by the holy rood !
A man all light, a seraph-man,   490
On every corse there stood.

This seraph-band, each waved his hand :
It was a heavenly sight !
They stood as signals to the land,
Each one a lovely light ;

This seraph-band, each waved his hand,
No voice did they impart—
No voice ; but O, the silence sank
Like music on my heart.

But soon I heard the dash of oars,   500
I heard the Pilot's cheer ;
My head was turn'd perforce away,
And I saw a boat appear.

The Pilot and the Pilot's boy,
I heard them coming fast :
Dear Lord in Heaven ! it was a joy
The dead men could not blast.

I saw a third—I heard his voice :
It is the Hermit good !
He singeth loud his godly hymns   510
That he makes in the wood.
He'll shrieve my soul, he'll wash away
The Albatross's blood.

Part VII.

" This hermit good lives in that wood   The Hermit
Which slopes down to the sea.   of the Wood.
How loudly his sweet voice he rears !
He loves to talk with mariners
That come from a far countree.

He kneels at morn, and noon, and eve—
He hath a cushion plump :   520
It is the moss that wholly hides
The rotted old oak-stump.

The skiff-boat near'd : I heard them talk,
' Why, this is strange, I trow !
Where are those lights so many and fair,
That signal made but now ? '

' Strange, by my faith ! ' the Hermit said—
'And they answer'd not our cheer !
The planks look warp'd ! and see those sails,
How thin they are and sere !   530
I never saw aught like to them,
Unless perchance it were
Brown skeletons of leaves that lag
My forest-brook along ;
When the ivy-tod is heavy with snow,
And the owlet whoops to the wolf below,
That eats the she-wolf's young.'

' Dear Lord ! it hath a fiendish look—
(The Pilot made reply)
I am a-fear'd.'—' Push on, push on ! '
Said the Hermit cheerily.   540

The boat came closer to the ship,
But I nor spake nor stirr'd ;
The boat came close beneath the ship,
And straight a sound was heard.

Under the water it rumbled on,
Still louder and more dread :
It reach'd the ship, it split the bay ;
The ship went down like lead.

Stunn'd by that loud and dreadful sound,   550
Which sky and ocean smote,
Like one that hath been seven days drown'd
My body lay afloat ;
But swift as dreams, myself I found
Within the Pilot's boat.

Upon the whirl, where sank the ship,
The boat spun round and round ;
And all was still, save that the hill
Was telling of the sound.

I moved my lips—the Pilot shriek'd   560
And fell down in a fit ;
The holy Hermit raised his eyes,
And pray'd where he did sit.

I took the oars : the Pilot's boy,
Who now doth crazy go,
Laugh'd loud and long, and all the while
His eyes went to and fro.
' Ha ! ha ! ' quoth he, ' full plain I see
The Devil knows how to row.'

And now, all in my own countree,   570
I stood on the firm land !
The Hermit stepp'd forth from the boat,
And scarcely he could stand.

' O shrieve me, shrieve me, holy man ! '
The Hermit cross'd his brow.
' Say quick,' quoth he, ' I bid thee say—
What manner of man art thou ? '

The ancient
Mariner
earnestly en-
treateth the
Hermit to
shrieve him ;
and the pen-
ance of life
alls on him.

Forthwith this frame of mine was wrench'd
With a woful agony,
Which forced me to begin my tale ;   580
And then it left me free.

Since then, at an uncertain hour,
That agony returns :
And till my ghastly tale is told,
This heart within me burns.

And ever and
anon through-
out his future
life an agony
constraineth
him to travel
from land to
land;

I pass, like night, from land to land ;
I have strange power of speech ;
That moment that his face I see,
I know the man that must hear me :
To him my tale I teach.   590

What loud uproar bursts from that door !
The wedding-guests are there :
But in the garden-bower the bride
And bride-maids singing are :
And hark, the little vesper bell,
Which biddeth me to prayer !

O Wedding-Guest ! this soul hath been
Alone on a wide, wide sea :
So lonely 'twas, that God Himself
Scarce seemèd there to be.   600

O sweeter than the marriage-feast,
'Tis sweeter far to me,
To walk together to the kirk
With a goodly company !—

To walk together to the kirk,
And all together pray,
While each to his great Father bends,
Old men, and babes, and loving friends,
And youths and maidens gay !

And to teach,
by his own
example, love
and reverence
to all things
that God made
and loveth.

Farewell, farewell ! but this I tell   610
To thee, thou Wedding-Guest !
He prayeth well, who loveth well
Both man and bird and beast.

He prayeth best, who loveth best
All things both great and small ;
For the dear God who loveth us,
He made and loveth all."

The Mariner, whose eye is bright,
Whose beard with age is hoar,
Is gone : and now the Wedding-Guest   620
Turn'd from the bridegroom's door.

He went like one that hath been stunn'd,
And is of sense forlorn :
A sadder and a wiser man
He rose the morrow morn.

NOTES

ALFRED, LORD TENNYSON (1809–1892)

MORTE D'ARTHUR.

ARTHUR, a Christian King of Britain, is supposed to have lived some time during the sixth century. For the purpose of repelling the attacks of the Saxon hordes and of redressing the abuses which had sprung up throughout his realm, he founded an order of knighthood known as the Round Table, the members of which vowed:

> ' To reverence the King, as if he were
> Their conscience, and their conscience as their King,
> To break the heathen and uphold the Christ,
> To ride abroad redressing human wrongs,
> To speak no slander, no, nor listen to it,
> To honour his own word as if his God's,
> To lead sweet lives in purest chastity,
> To love one maiden only, cleave to her,
> And worship her by years of noble deeds
> Until they won her.'

But dissension and treachery dissolved the order, and after the final battle Sir Bedivere alone of the knights remained, while Arthur himself, was mortally wounded.

Tennyson tells the whole story of Arthur's life in the *Idylls of the King*, a series of twelve poems almost great enough to be regarded as an epic. The *Morte d'Arthur*, the first of the twelve to be written, became, with additions, the last of the series under the title *The Passing of Arthur*. The poet used Sir Thomas Malory's prose version of the Arthurian legends, which was printed by Caxton in 1472, as the basis of his work, and the student is urged to read, side by side with the poem, Malory's account of the 'last weird battle in the West and the Passing of Arthur.'

 4. **Lyonnesse** : according to tradition, a tract of land, now submerged, between Land's End and the Scilly Isles.

14. **The sequel of to-day**: the result of to-day's battle, in which all Arthur's knights but the bold Sir Bedivere had been slain.

21. **Camelot**: Arthur's capital. Like most of the place-names in the *Idylls*, it cannot be identified with anything like certainty, and Tennyson's poetical description of it in *The Holy Grail* does nothing to assist in its identification, any more than does its prominence in *The Lady of Shalott*.

23. **Merlin**: the great enchanter, who had made Arthur King.

27. **Excalibur**: Arthur's marvellous sword, given to him by the Lady of the Lake.

31. **samite**: a kind of rich silk stuff. This fine line is twice repeated (ll. 144, 159).

37. **into the middle mere**: a Latin idiom—*in medium mare*. **him**: note how, here and elsewhere, the sword is spoken of as a living thing.

43. **hest**: behest, command.

49-51. Note here, as elsewhere in this poem (*e.g.*, ll. 70, 71 and 186-192) the skill with which Tennyson weds *sound* with *sense*.

57. **topaz**: a precious stone, found in great variety of colour. The colour of the *jacinth* is reddish-purple.

60. An almost literal translation of a line of Virgil (*Æneid*, VIII. 20).

80. **lief**: true, dear; now used as an adverb=gladly.

110. **clouded with his own conceit**: i.e., his thoughts prevented him from seeing clearly his duties as a true knight.

116, 117. Note this repetition of his previous answer (ll. 70, 71), slightly varied.

121-3. A dying King, bereft of the power which formerly compelled obedience by a mere look, can no longer exercise authority.

139. **a streamer of the northern morn**: the arch of lights known as the Aurora Borealis. This electrical phenomenon is best seen in northern latitudes, though it has been observed as far south as the Thames. The whole passage is a splendid piece of figurative description.

140. **moving isles of winter**: icebergs.

147. Contrast the lilt of this line with the heaviness of ll. 65 and 112 above.

182. **clothed with his breath**: his breath condensed into a mist, which enveloped him as he went.

193. **hove**: hove in sight, or, perhaps, lay at anchor.

199. Note how appropriate the word ' shiver'd ' is. In the cold winter's night the cry of the Queens is regarded as making the stars tingle.

202, 203. Note the sense of desolation expressed by these two lines.

F*

215. greaves, cuisses : armour for the legs and thighs respectively.

215-16. drops of onset : blood shed in the battle.

221. A column is typical of strength. Cp. Scott, *Marmion*, Introduction to Canto First :

> ' Now is the stately column broke.'

232-3. See St. Matthew ii. 9-11.

240-2. Words of comfort to the sorrowing knight. In His dealings with man God does not allow any method, however good it may be, to become stale and profitless through disregard due to constant repetition. The whole passage (ll. 240-264) is full of beautiful and striking lines, many of which have become almost proverbial.

255. Prayers are the gold chains which bind the world round the feet of God.

259. Avilion : or Avalon, a Celtic name which means ' the island of apples.' Either Glastonbury, in Somerset, where, according to tradition, Arthur was buried, or, it may be, some isle of the western ocean, like the ' Fortunate Islands ' of the Greeks.

260-4. Cp. Tennyson's *Lucretius* :

> ' The lucid interspace of world and world,
>   Where never creeps a cloud or moves a wind,
>   Nor ever falls the least white star of snow,
>   Nor ever lowest roll of thunder moans,
>   Nor sound of human sorrow mounts to mar
>   Their sacred, everlasting calm !

and Swinburne, *Atalanta in Calydon :*

> ' Lands indiscoverable in the unheard-of west,
>   Round which the strong stream of a sacred sea
>   Rolls without wind for ever, and the snow
>   There shows not her white wings and windy feet,
>   Nor thunder nor swift rain saith anything,
>   Nor the sun burns, but all things rest and thrive.

All three passages are based on the description of Olympus in Homer's *Odyssey*, VI.43-45, thus translated by Butcher and Lang : ' Not by winds is it shaken, nor ever wet with rain, nor doth the snow come nigh thereto, but most clear air is spread about it cloudless, and the white light floats over it.'

262. deep meadowed : having meadows with long rich grass.

263. *i.e.*, tree-girt valleys, beyond which lies the unruffled and brightly gleaming sea.

266. **Just before its death a swan was supposed to sing.** This belief is
referred to by Shakespeare and many other poets—*e.g., The
Merchant of Venice*, III. ii. :

> ' Then, if he lose, he makes a swan-like end,
> Fading in music ' ;

and Byron, *The Isles of Greece :*

> ' There, swan-like, let me sing and die.'

MATTHEW ARNOLD (1822–1888)

SOHRAB AND RUSTUM.

This spirited poem is based on an ' episode ' in a Persian epic dealing
with the early legends of that country. Rustum is the Persian national
hero, who spent his life in driving back the Mongol hordes of Tartary in
their frequent attacks on his native land. The poem itself explains how
Rustum's son Sohrab came to be fighting on the side of Afrasiab, King of
the Tartars, against his father and his countrymen. Most of the Oriental
names, so numerous in the early part of the poem, are of little importance
except to give the necessary atmosphere, and need not be identified.
The style, as befits the story, is simple and direct, embellished only by a
series of elaborate similes, modelled on those of Homer.

2. **the Oxus :** a river of great importance in antiquity, as it formed the
boundary between the Persians and the nomadic Tartar tribes. Its
modern name is the Amu Daria, and it now flows into the Sea of
Aral, but most probably it emptied itself into the Caspian Sea.
On its banks the rival Persian and Tartar hosts are, at the open-
ing of the poem, encamped.

15. **high Pamere :** the Pamir plateau, North of India, where the Oxus.
rises.

38. **Afrasiab :** King of the Tartars, who invaded Persia three times.

40. **Samarcand :** see note on *Eve of St. Agnes*, Stanza XXX.

42. **Ader-baijan, Seistan** (l. 82) and **Khorassan** (l. 138) are Persian
provinces.

113. **Casbin :** or Kazvin, town south of the Elburz range.

114. **Elburz :** mountains in North of Persia, south of the Caspian.

119. **Bokhara :** a province of Turkestan (so also **Khiva** and **Ferghana**),
bordered on the south by the Oxus, between Samarcand and
Afghanistan. Sheep (cp. l. 101) still form one of the principal
sources of the province's wealth.

In the following we have a list of the various tribes of Turkestan of which the Tartar army was composed.

129. **Jaxartes :** now Sir Daria, which flows into the north of the Sea of Aral.

160. **Cabool** or Kabul, the capital of Afghanistan.

161. **underneath :** from below.

the Indian Caucasus : the Hindu Kush range.

162. **sky-neighbouring :** cp. *Hamlet*, III. iv. : ' a heaven-kissing hill.'

217. **Iran :** old name of Persia.

223. **Kai Khosroo :** Cyrus the elder, founder of the Persian Empire, the history of whose life was wrapped in romance. The story of his capturing Babylon by turning the course of the Euphrates is well known.

233. **vex :** harass.

268. **spine :** here=peak or crest.

277. **dight :** adorned.

284-290. A typical simile of Matthew Arnold, who frequently, as here, paints a complete but almost entirely detached picture of remarkable beauty, very like the similes of Homer.

286. **sandy Bahrein :** islands in the Persian Gulf, one of the chief centres for pearl-fishing, and under British protection for over half a century.

288. **tale :** number. A Saxon word ; cp. tally, to tell one's beads.

293. **swathe :** or swath, a row of mown grass.

390-397. Note these fine and striking lines.

412. **Hyphasis, Hydaspes :** the Sutlej and the Jhelum, tributaries of the Indus.

414. **wrack :** same as ' rack ' and ' wreck.'

452. **that autumn star :** Sirius, the most important star in the Great Dog constellation. Classical authors constantly apply the epithet ' baleful ' to Sirius because of the great heat and consequent unhealthiness of the Dies Caniculares, or Dog-days. But July is scarcely an autumn month !

458. **minion :** pampered favourite ; from Fr. *mignon*.

497. **shore :** old past of ' shear.'

502. Ruksh's dreadful cry can be paralleled from Homer and from Scott (*vide Battle of Bannockburn*, 1 175) ; but it would be difficult to cite a counterpart to the curdling of Oxus (l. 508).

556-575. Another thoroughly Homeric simile.

570. **glass :** an unusual use of the verb with a transitive sense, as 'mirror' is commonly used.

679. **griffin** : a fabulous animal, having the body of a lion, and the head and wings of an eagle. The figure was much used for ornamental purposes in Babylonian and Persian art. Both in mythology and in heraldry the griffin was presented with erect ears, symbolic of its guarding hidden gold.

751. **Helmund** : a river in Afghanistan.

861. **Jemshid** : or Jamshyd, ' King Splendid,' the reputed founder of Persepolis. Cp. Fitzgerald, *Rubaiyat of Omar Khayyam* :

> ' They say the Lion and the Lizard keep
> The Courts where Jamshyd gloried and drank deep.'

Persepolis : once the capital city of the Persian Empire. In his *Alexander's Feast* Dryden tells how Alexander, after his defeat of the Persians at Arbela in 331 B.C., entered Persepolis and gave up its accumulated treasure to be plundered by his soldiers, he himself, at the instigation of Thais, setting fire to the royal palace.

878. **Chorasmian waste** : marsh-land and islands in the lower course of the Oxus.

889-892. Note the beauty and calm of the closing lines, corresponding to that of the opening lines, and contrasting with the tragic intensity of the fight.

HENRY WADSWORTH LONGFELLOW (1807-1882)

OSSEO AND OWEENEE.

At the wedding-feast of Hiawatha and Minnehaha, Iagoo, old and ugly the marvellous story-teller, tells this ' tale of wonder.' The metre is trochaic tetrameter, a simple but spirited measure, admirably adapted to the simplicity of the Indian legends embodied in the poem. There is no rime, but instead a good deal of what has been called *parallelism*—viz.: a repetition in successive lines either of words or of the same idea in different words, as is common in the Psalms and other ancient poetry.

7. **lithe** : supple and graceful.

23. **the Evening Star** : Venus.

31. **wampum** : small shells, strung together and elaborately embroidered on pieces of deer-skin, formed the principal adornment among the Indians.

127. **doom** : curse.

136. **whippoorwill** : probably an imitative name. The bird is a species of swallow.

153. **shards :** wing-cases. Shakespeare applies the epithets 'shard borne' and 'sharded' to the noun 'beetle.'
262. **the Big-Sea-Water :** Gitche Gumee—*i.e.*, Lake Superior.
278. **the Puk-Wudjies :** the Little People, like Puck and the fairies in Shakespeare's *Midsummer Night's Dream.*

SIR WALTER SCOTT (1771–1832)

THE BATTLE OF BANNOCKBURN.

Scott's narrative poems provide us with two superlative battle-pieces, companion pictures of well-nigh equal excellence—his descriptions of Flodden Field in *Marmion* and of Bannockburn in *The Lord of the Isles.* The metre is iambic tetrameter, with varying rimes, the couplet being the most common, and occasional shorter lines of three feet.

1. The battle was fought on June 24, 1314. On the previous day took place the combat between the King and De Boune, described in xiii.-xv.
3. **Demayet :** a peak in the Ochil Hills, N.E. of Stirling, the last and most important of the Scottish fortresses which held out for Edward of England.
12. **frequent corse :** numerous corpses. A Latin idiom.
16. **wassail :** an adjective=drunken.
22. So, in the case of Flodden, Clare watched the progress of the battle from a hillock.
30. **bittern :** a bird of the heron family which utters a booming note.
41. **battalia :** the main battle-line.
71, 72. The Abbot of Inchaffray, after celebrating Mass, blessed the Scottish army.
77. **Earl Gilbert :** 'Gloster's Earl' of the preceding line.
96. **fell :** cruel, deadly.
110. **rest :** the support in which the butt-end of the lance reposed.
117. **to let :** to stem or impede.
131. **Sherwood** Forest : in Nottinghamshire.
135-9. A reference to English May-Day sports.
144. **wight :** adjective=sturdy, strong and bold. Cp. *Marmion*, VI. **xx.**:

'O for one hour of Wallace wight !'

146. **baldric :** belt, girdle.
171. **acton :** a leathern vest worn under the coat of mail.
175. The poet justifies this line in a note.

196. **Falkirk**, 1296. *Methven*, 1306. *Dunbar*, 1296. **All** well-known battles in Scottish history.

198. **Cressy** : *Crecy*, 1346 ; *Poitiers*, 1356. Victories won by Edward III and the Black Prince against the French.

236. **inn** : *i.e.*, home. Cp. Fitzgerald, *Rubaiyat of Omar Khayyam* :

> ' Think, in this battered caravanserai,
> Whose doorways are alternate night and **day.**'

259. **Ailsa Rock** : Ailsa Craig, in the Firth of Clyde.

261. **Carrick** : a district in the south of the modern county of **Ayr**, where Bruce had property.

268. **sons of Innisgail** : *i.e.*, Highlanders, the sons of the islands of the Gael.

295. The camp-followers on Gillies Hill in the rear.

300. **clerk** : cleric of inferior rank.

303. **mute Amadine** : Edith, in the guise of a mute page-boy called Amadine.

319. **wearied war** : dispirited troops.

322. **amain** : usually=with force or strength ; here=in a body (Fr. *a main*).

332. **caitiff** : cowardly.

338. **gage** : Argentine had given Bruce his glove, demanding ' redress of honour at thy hand ' (see *Lord of the Isles*, III. v.).

361. **Colonsay** : one of the Hebrides, W. of Jura.

369. **cuish** : armour-piece for protection of the thigh. In the *Morte d'Arthur* Tennyson uses the etymologically more **exact** form, ' cuisses.'

411. **Ninian** : St. Ninian was the earliest (fifth century A.D.) missionary to Scotland. A village between Stirling and Bannockburn bears his name.

412. **late-wake** : more correctly, *lyk*-wake, *i.c.*, watching by a corpse. Cp. *lich*-gate.

425. **leopards on thy shield** : Edward I. had as his device three leopards on his shield ; hence he was known as ' the English Leopard.'

GEORGE CRABBE (1754–1832)

RICHARD'S WOOING.

This poem is taken from the *Tales of the Hall*, the last great literary work of the once poor country surgeon of Norfolk who took Orders and was rector of Trowbridge in Wiltshire for almost twenty years.

Richard is the younger of two half-brothers, who, after spending his youth at sea, made a happy love marriage and found himself the poor father of a family of little children. George, the elder brother, has remained a bachelor, and, after a successful business career in London, has settled down to spend the rest of his days as squire of Binning Hall in the village of his boyhood. The brothers had seen little of each other; but now Richard pays a lengthy visit to Binning Hall and is received with a hearty welcome by George, who has begun to find his life a dull one. They wile away the weeks of the visit by telling stories of their lives. In this poem Richard gives the history of his earlier life; and in return we have *The Squire's Love-Story*.

The metre of Crabbe's narrative poems is the heroic couplet, so named because of its employment by translators of Greek and Latin epics—*e.g.*, by Dryden in his translation of Virgil's *Æneid*, and by Pope in his versions of Homer's *Iliad* and *Odyssey*. Note how the sense ends with the couplet and does not overflow into the next. If, as rarely, it does not so end, the couplet is expanded into a triplet, as in ll. 112 and 236. This convention, however, is not always observed when the metre is used in narrative poetry.

9-13. See *The Squire's Love-Story*.

18. **Their different states** : Richard, a poor man ; George, the wealthy owner of Binning Hall.

37-77. **A good instance** of Crabbe's great defect as a narrative poet—a diffuseness which clogs his tale.

60. **th' immortal Swede** : Linnæus, the celebrated Swedish botanist (1707-1778), the greatest of whose manifold services to natural science was the systematizing of the work of earlier botanists. His love of *order* was greater than his love of *nature*, and to this fact we owe his artificial classification of plants, without which, however, the scientific development of botany would have been almost impossible.

63. **a genus** is a group of **species**, all of which have common characteristics apart from those possessed by all other groups.

64. **sounding** : imposing, stately, as Latin botanical terms are.

71. The horse-fly and the swallow.

144. **white** : used figuratively=innocent, perfect.

153-159. Crabbe always loved to hear the sound of ' that old familiar sea which (with all its sad associations) the poet never liked to leave far behind him.'

191. **art** : artifice, craft, a meaning more prominent in the adjective ' artful.'

237. whatever is, is best: an echo of Pope (cp. *Essay on Man*, last line in the first epistle). ' Crabbe was born and bred too soon ever to divest himself entirely, like Wordsworth, of that eighteenth-century pseudo-classic style and diction which rings so untrue in our ears ' (Bernard Holland).

WILLIAM WORDSWORTH (1770–1850)

MICHAEL.

Wordsworth's gifts were lyrical and reflective rather than narrative. As he himself says in *Hart-Leap Well* :

' The moving accident is not my trade,'

but rather

' To pipe a simple song for thinking hearts.'

Michael is one of his few narrative poems. As such it lacks life and movement, but it is a good example of the poet's human sympathy and simple, natural style.

2. Ghyll : a variant form of *gill*, a wooded dell or ravine. An Icelandic word.

5. pastoral mountains : mountains on which shepherds tend their flocks. *Michael* is a pastoral poem—*i.e.*, a tale of shepherds in which much is told of country life in general, and in which description of country scenery abounds. Cp. ll. 21-26.

11. kites : birds of prey of the hawk type.

17. unhewn : not dressed by the mason and therefore of irregular shape.

35. rude : simple, guileless, free from all that is artificial.

36. natural hearts : simple-minded people.

90. telling o'er : counting.

102. a mess of pottage : probably oatmeal porridge. A *mess* is a dish of food. The same word is applied to a company of persons, especially in the Army or Navy, who take their meals together *Mess*, meaning a disagreeable mixture, is quite a different word. *Pottage* is food cooked in a *pot*.

108. to card wool (or flax) is to comb out the strands.

110. flail : a primitive threshing implement, consisting of a bar of wood fastened by a hinge to a long handle.

113. uncouth : rough, unpolished, and hence odd.

141. The Evening Star : Wordsworth's note runs : ' The sheepfold, on which so much of the poem turns, remains, or rather the ruins of it. The character and circumstances of Luke were taken from a family to which had belonged, many years before, the house we lived in at Town-end [Grasmere], along with some fields and woodlands on the eastern shore of Grasmere. The name of the Evening Star was not in fact given to this house, but to another on the same side of the valley, more to the north.'

146, 147. **The same . . . of all** : *i.e.*, the natural instinct of parental love.

155. **female service** : the duties towards a child usually performed by the mother.

170. **The Clipping Tree** : ' Clipping ' is the word still used in the North of England for ' shearing.'

191, 192. *i.e.*, his father did not always give him praise as wages for work done.

202. **emanations** : sentiments—such as love for his father—which flowed from the boy.

211, 212. The shepherd had legally bound himself to pay off his nephew's creditors, ' to discharge the forfeiture,' if the nephew should fail to do so.

217. **But** is an adverb.

225. **patrimonial fields** : the fields which he has inherited from his father. Cp. Pope, *Ode on Solitude* :

> ' Happy the man whose wish and care
> A few paternal acres bound.'

260. **a parish-boy** : a pauper, reared at the expense of the parish.

267. **overlook** : supervise. Cp. the noun *overseer*.

371. *i.e.*, to be laid to rest in the family burial-ground.

375. **burthened** : the burden was a mortgage—*i.e.*, money had been raised on the security of the land, and the payment of the interest was a first charge on the income derived from it.

391. **hale** : healthy and vigorous. *Whole* is etymologically the same word.

WILLIAM MORRIS (1834–1896)

ATALANTA'S RACE.

The *Earthly Paradise*, from which this poem is taken, is modelled on Chaucer's *Canterbury Tales*, in so far, at any rate, as it consists of a Prologue, twenty-four tales—two for each month in the year—and an Epilogue. Twelve of the tales are classical in origin ; the other twelve are romantic.

Atalanta was as an infant exposed by her father, King Schœneus, and was reared by a she-bear. When she grew up to womanhood and her father desired her to marry, she made it a condition that any suitor for her hand should contend with her in the footrace, and in the case of failure should be put to death. The poem tells of the victory of Milanion with the assistance of Venus.

The stanza used in this poem is the septette, generally known as the Rime Royal, because of its employment by James I. of Scotland in his *King's Quair*. Morris was a devoted disciple of Chaucer, and he revived this delightful measure of his master for longer narrative poems. The metre is iambic pentameter, riming *ababbcc*.

STANZA I. **Argolis** : in N.E. Peloponnesus (Morea), where, however, the goddess worshipped was Hera, and not Aphrodite.

he : Milanion, son of King Amphidamas, who was waiting for the month to expire before the day appointed for his trial in speed with Atalanta.

lion-bearing lands : probably Africa, hence the line=facing south.

close-clipped : from ' to clip '=to hold tightly, to squeeze. The noun is in everyday use.

murk : the residue after grapes have been pressed and all the juice extracted from them. Fr. *marc*=dregs, lees.

STANZA III. **image** : the marble statue of Venus.

STANZA V. **the Sea-born One** : Aphrodite (Venus), of whom the later Greek poets sang that she was born of the sea-foam, off the coast of Cyprus.

STANZA X. **The golden age** : the fabulous reign of Saturn, who was reputed to have introduced civilisation and agriculture, the source of real wealth, into Italy, with the result that the country was called Saturnia, the land of plenty. Cp. Milton, *Ode on Christ's Nativity* :

' Time will run back and fetch the age of gold.'

STANZA XV. **nought, nothing** : nouns used adverbially. So, too, *aught* in the next stanza.

STANZA XXVI. l. 2—*i.e.*, that she will consent to marry you. Diana was the virgin goddess and special protectress of maidens.

Saturn's clime : see note on Stanza X.

STANZA XL. **Argive** : properly inhabitant of Argos, reputed the oldest city in Greece and the nucleus of the chief state in the Peloponnesus, of which in Homer's time Mycenæ was capital and Agamemnon King ; hence, as here=Greek.

STANZA XLIII. Her joy is due, not merely to the change in her own heart, but also to the fact that at last the curse has been lifted from the land.

JOHN KEATS (1795–1821)

THE EVE OF ST. AGNES.

St. Agnes was a Roman maiden who was martyred at the age of twelve during the fierce persecution of Christians in A.D. 303 by the Emperor Diocletian. Her festival is January 21st, and her symbol is a lamb. She was the patron-saint of love-sick maidens, and those who on her Eve went to bed fasting were supposed to see their future husbands in a dream.

The poem is written in the Spenserian stanza, so called because Spenser was the first poet to use it. It consists of eight iambic pentameters rounded off with an Alexandrine (iambic hexameter), the whole riming *ababbcbcc*.

STANZA I. a-cold : an intensive form of the adjective, used also by Shakespeare in *King Lear*, III. iv. 57. Note how, in this stanza, Keats makes us *feel* the intense mid-winter cold, and cp. for this Milton's sonnet *On the Late Massacre in Piedmont.*

Beadsman : lit. prayersman ; usually a pensioner who offers regular prayers for his benefactor.

STANZA II. meagre : having little flesh on his bones, and being consequently feeble.

the sculptur'd dead . . . : the monuments to the dead, adorned with figures in stone of knights and ladies in an attitude of prayer, are separated from the chapel aisle by black rails. Here and again in the last three lines of Stanza IV. we see Keats's wonderful powers of description by which he seems to make the works of sculpture *live*.

STANZA IV. to chide : to utter shrill notes.

level : implies extent as well as smoothness. Cp. *Morte d'Arthur*, ll. 51, 191.

STANZA V. revelry : the riotous merry-makers.

STANZA VI. Here we have the pivot of the poem—the conditions under which, on St. Agnes' Eve, a maiden might dream of her future lover.

supine : lying on the back ; opposed to ' prone.'

STANZA VII. tiptoe : an adjective, expressing the eager anticipation with which the cavalier approached Madeline.

STANZA VIII. amort : unconscious, dead to the world ; Fr. à mort.

her lambs : a lamb (Lat. *agnus*) is the emblem of the saint.

STANZA IX. Porphyro belongs to a hostile house, as the next stanza shows. Cp. *Romeo and Juliet.*

STANZA x. **beldame** : merely an old woman. So Shakespeare speaks of
' old beldame earth.'

STANZA XII. **Gossip** : cp. use of Fr. *commère*.

STANZA XIII. '**St. Agnes' wool** is that shorn from two lambs which
(allusive to the Saint's name) were upon that day brought to Mass
and offered while the *Agnus* was chanted. The wool was then
spun, dressed, and woven by the hand of nuns ' (Palgrave).

STANZA XIV. **a witch's sieve** was supposed to hold or keep out water.
Cp. *Macbeth*, I. iii., where the First Witch says :

' In a sieve I'll thither sail.'

STANZA XV. **brook**, usually = endure ; here = restrain.

STANZA XVI. **made purple riot** : stirred passionate emotion.

STANZA XVIII. **passing-bell** : bell tolled for the dying, possibly to frighten
off evil spirits.

plaining : complaining, lamenting.

STANZA XIX. The exact meaning of Merlin's **monstrous debt** is not quite
clear ; but Keats seems to imply a bargain, like that between
Mephistopheles and Faust, under which Merlin pledged his soul to
the Devil in return for the magical powers bestowed on him. For
the usual version of Merlin's end see the closing lines of Tennyson's
Merlin and Vivien or of Matthew Arnold's *Tristram and Iseult*.

STANZA XX. **cates** : delicacies ; connected with verb ' cater ' and Fr.
acheter, achat.

tambour frame : circular frame on which material is stretched while
it is being embroidered.

STANZA XXII. **balustrade** : a row of short shaped pillars with rail or
coping, the whole forming an ornamental parapet to a balcony

l. 4. Only after repeated attempts did the poet achieve this exquisite
line.

fray'd : frightened.

ring-dove is another name for the cushat, or wood-pigeon.

STANZA XXIV. A magnificent piece of description, full of gorgeous colour-
ing, especially ll. 5 and 6, and in the final or Alexandrine. This,
too, was attained only after much care and labour.

knot-grass : a common weed with intricately knotted stem and
flowers of a pale pink hue.

shielded scutcheon : escutcheon or shield with coat of arms.

blush'd : dyed, crimsoned.

STANZA XXV. Another wonderful stanza, though, as Sir Sidney Colvin
remarks, ' observation shows that moonlight has not the power to
transmit the hues of painted glass.'

gules : the heraldic term for red.

amethyst : a bluish-violet colour.

STANZA XXVI. warmèd jewels : as though the warmth of Madeline's body
had been transferred to them.

STANZA XXVII. poppied : opium is distilled from the poppy. Hence
sleep is regarded as a narcotic that soothes her wearied limbs.
Cp. Swinburne, *Ilicet* :

' The end of all, the poppied sleep.'

missal : a Roman Catholic prayer-book, often richly illuminated.

swart Paynims : dark-skinned heathen.

l. 7. Cherished for itself and for the danger of having it in a pagan
land.

STANZA XXIX. Morphean amulet : sleep charm. Morpheus, the son of
Sleep, was the god of dreams.

affray : jar on ; archaic use of the word, now employed only as a
noun.

STANZA XXX. Another masterpiece of description. ' We are made to feel
how those ideal and rare sweets of sense surround and minister to
her, not only with their own natural richness, but with the
associations and the homage of all far countries whence they have
been gathered ' (Colvin).

soother : seems used for smoother or softer.

tinct : flavoured.

Fez : the capital of Morocco.

Samarcand : a town in Western Turkestan, which in the twelfth and
early thirteenth centuries had half a million inhabitants and was
the chief city of Central Asia. Though now much decayed, it has
still a brisk trade in cotton, silk, and fruit.

Lebanon : a mountain range in Syria, formerly covered with a great
forest of cedars, of which Solomon built his Temple (*vide*
1 Kings v. 6, 7). Of these only a few groves remain ; but there
are forests of oak, pine, plane, cypress, and other trees.

STANZA XXXI. eremite : same word as hermit ; used also by the poet in
his last sonnet, beginning :

' Bright star ! would I were steadfast as thou art.'

STANZA XXXII. entoil'd in woofèd phantasies : under the spell of fancies
interwoven with one another.

STANZA XXXIII. Provence : South-East France, the home of the trouba-
dours and land of music and song.

La belle dame sans mercy : the title of a French poem by Alain

Chartier, Court poet to Charles VII. of France in the fifteenth century. In 1819 Keats wrote his famous ballad with this title.

STANZA XXXVI. **solution** : here = mingling.

Note in the last lines the suggestion of the cold without, in sharp contrast to the warmth within.

STANZA XXXVII. **flaw-blown** : a *flaw* is a sudden gust of wind, like the American ' flurry.'

STANZA XXXVIII. **vermeil** : vermilion, bright red.

STANZA XXXIX. **Rhenish** : Rhine wine.

mead : a drink of fermented honey and water.

STANZA XL. **darkling** : in the dark—a favourite epithet of Keats.

arras : tapestry. From Arras, in the North of France, between Lille and Amiens.

l. 9. The mention of carpets is an anachronism.

STANZA XLI. Note throughout this stanza how wonderfully the sound is wedded to the sense.

owns : recognizes.

STANZA XLII. The death of the Beadsman is foreshadowed in Stanza III. ; that of Angela in Stanza XVIII.

be-nightmared : a word coined by Keats.

deform : misshapen ; Lat. *deformis*.

aves : an *Ave Maria* is a prayer to the Virgin.

The bitter cold and storm, with which the poem opens, and of which we are reminded in Stanza XXXVI., recur in this closing stanza, and the poem ends with the same note on which it began, one very appropriate to the 20th of January.

GEORGE GORDON, LORD BYRON (1788–1824)

MAZEPPA.

Byron has modelled this vigorous poem on the account given by Voltaire in his history of Charles XII. of Sweden. Mazeppa is an old soldier, Hetman of the Ukraine Cossacks, who tells the tale of his youth to the wounded and fugitive Charles after his disastrous defeat by the Russians at Pultowa in 1709.

> ' " I request,"
> Said Sweden's monarch, " thou wilt tell
> This tale of thine, and I may reap,
> Perchance, from this the boon of sleep ;
> For at this moment from my eyes
> The hope of present slumber flies."

The tale is certainly not one to induce sleep in the listener, but

> ' If ye marvel Charles forgot
> To thank his tale, *he* wondered not—
> The King had been an hour asleep.'

The metre is similar to that employed by Scott in his metrical romances.

STANZA IX. As a punishment for having made love to a Polish countess, Mazeppa was bound on the back of an untamed Tartar horse, which was then turned loose.

Ukraine : the region of the middle Dnieper valley, sometimes called Little Russia, inhabited by Cossacks whose principal industries are agriculture, cattle- and horse-breeding. Kiev and Kharkov are the chief towns. The name has recently come into considerable prominence in connection with the Russian Revolution.

STANZA X. rabble rout : noisy, disorderly crowd.

portcullis : a sliding or falling gate.

STANZA XI. meteors : fire-balls or shooting-stars.

northern light : the aurora borealis. Whether any crackling sound (apart from the splitting up of icebergs) accompanies the display of the aurora is at least open to question.

Tartars : the original Dnieper Cossacks may themselves have been Tartars.

Spahi : irregular Turkish cavalryman. Cp. Indian ' Sepoy.'

STANZA XII. scarr'd with cold : the cold had closed his wounds with rough scars.

a rood : in linear measure generally called a rod (pole or perch), 5½ yards in length ; but used here loosely by Byron, who evidently means a greater distance.

STANZA XIII. he who dies . . . I died : Mazeppa endured all the agonies of actual death.

STANZA XIV. hollow trance : hollow, because in it all he saw seemed unreal.

STANZA XV. ignis-fatuus : a will-o'-the-wisp, a misleading light which scientists attribute to the presence of marsh gas.

STANZA XVI. dapple : unusual in this meaning.

STANZA XVII. insect's shrill small horn : Milton (*Lycidas*, 28) speaks of the gray-fly winding her horn—*i.e.*, making a loud humming noise.

matin bird : *i.e.*, bird in the early morning.

werst : a Russian mile=3,500 English feet ; usually written verst.

inevitable : **death,** which cannot be avoided. So, too, in Gray's
Elegy, ' the inevitable hour.'

wassail : a corruption of A.S. *wes hal,* ' may you be in good health.'
A carousal. In Frisia, the old home of the English, it is said that
newcomers at an inn are greeted to this day by the guests already
present with the words ' Wæs hial ! '

guerdon : recompense, reward ; lit. war-gift (Fr. *guerre*+*don*).

STANZA XIX. **her due return** : her return at the fitting time.

STANZA XX. **one day . . . to reign** : Mazeppa became the ' hetman '
(*i.e.,* headman) of the band.

Borysthenes : the Dnieper.

ROBERT BROWNING (1812–1889)

PHEIDIPPIDES.

The story comes originally from Herodotus, who tells us how, when the
Persians invaded Attica, the great runner was sent from Athens to Sparta
to ask aid against the common enemy. He covered the distance, 150
miles, in two days ; but the superstitious Spartans, none too anxious to
save their rivals, said that they could not set out before the full moon.
Pheidippides, disgusted and indignant, immediately started back, and
met on his way the god Pan, who foretold victory for the Athenians and
for the runner a worthy reward. He arrived (another tradition tells us)
in time to fight at Marathon ; and, when the battle was won, was called
upon to run once more, this time to carry the good news to Athens. He
responded immediately, burst into the market-place with ' Victory ! ' on
his lips, and then dropped down dead from exhaustion, thus gaining the
promised reward—the glorious death of a hero.

The poem is in stanzas of eight lines, the rime scheme being *abcddcab.*
The scansion is far from easy. On a first reading—at least, to anyone
accustomed to classical metres—the poem seems composed in dactylic
hexameters with the last syllable cut off ; the so-called hexameter
catalectic. But a more careful study reveals the apparent hexameters as
six-foot anapæsts, usually based on a monosyllabic first and with frequent
iambic substitution—a metrical scheme which, if somewhat fantastic,
seems to suit the rush and hurry of the poem. Accordingly, the first four
lines scan as follows :

' First | I salute | this soil | of the bless|ed riv|er and rock !
Gods | of my birth | place, dæ | mons and he|roes, hon|our to all !
Then | I name thee, | claim thee | for our pa|tron co-e|qual in praise
—Ay, | with Zeus | the defend|er, with Her|of the æ|gis and spear ! '

There is, however, a batch of four lines (20-23) which contain seven feet each, thus doubtless simulating the rapid utterance of the excited and breathless runner, and also a single line (63) and two successive lines (87, 88) of similar length.

Two other poems of Browning, *Abt Vogler* and *Muleykeh*, are in practically the same metre.

2. **dæmons** : spirits who occupy a place between gods and men : inferior deities.

4 **Zeus** : the greatest of the Olympian gods. In later mythology the Romans identified their Jupiter with the Greek Zeus.

Her of the ægis : Athene, one of the twelve great Olympian deities, and daughter of Zeus, from whose forehead she was said to have issued in full armour. So, as goddess of war, she was usually represented, the ægis being her shield, in the centre of which was the head of the Gorgon Medusa. She was the special protectress of Athens, which was called, after her, Athenæ.

5 **Ye of the bow and the buskin** : Apollo (in his character as the god who *punishes*) and his twin-sister Artemis, the huntress. The buskin was a kind of high boot, reaching to the calf or even to the knees.

8. **Pan** : originally the Arcadian god of flocks and shepherds. His worship was introduced among the Athenians at the time of the battle of Marathon. He is represented in works of art as half man, half goat, with goat's horns, beard, tail, legs, and hoofs (*vide* ll. 66, 68, 69).

9. **Archons** : the name given to the nine chief magistrates at Athens.

tettix : a gold ornament in the shape of a grasshopper, worn by the archons as the national emblem.

11. **myrtle** : Among the Greeks the myrtle was the symbol of youth and beauty, and myrtle wreaths were worn at festivals.

18. **water and earth** : it was customary for conquerors to demand these as tokens of submission.

19. **Eretria** : a town on the west coast of Eubœa (mod. Negropont).

31. **quarry** : really the object of pursuit of a bird or beast of prey ; hence a victim. From Fr. *cuir*, Lat. *corium*, hide. The entrails of the deer used to be put on a hide and given to hounds.

32. **Phoibus** : ' the bright '—*i.e.*, Apollo.

33. **Olumpos** : a mountain-range in the north of Greece, the favourite abode of Zeus and the other immortal gods.

37-40. The Spartans were not sorry to know of the plight of Athens, and so made the excuse that they could not undertake an expedition until the moon was full. Then they set out, but arrived too late, after Marathon had been won.

47. filleted victim : the temples of sacrificial victims were bound with a
   chaplet or garland called a ' fillet.'

   libation : an offering of wine (or other liquid) poured out in honour
   of a deity ; **fulsome,** because offered in an offensively cringing
   spirit.

52. Parnes : a well-wooded mountain range in the north of Attica, the
   vineyards on whose lower slopes yield a favourite wine. Browning's
   geography is at fault, for Mount Parnes does not lie on the direct
   route run by Pheidippides, but is several miles north of it.
   Herodotus says that Pan appeared to the runner on Mount
   Parthenium, which is on the borders of Arcadia. As the Arcadians
   were hunters and shepherds, they naturally worshipped Pan.

62 Erebos : according to the Greeks, a dark cavern beneath the earth,
   through which the shades passed on their way to Hades.

66. wanton : in unrestrained profusion.

80. greaved-thigh : *i.e.*, the Athenian soldiers, with their leg armour.

83. Fennel : an aromatic plant common in the south of Europe. The
   name Marathon was supposed to mean ' fennel-field ' (*vide* l. 109).

87. on the razor's edge : in extreme danger ; a Greek expression.

89. Miltiades : the Greek leader at Marathon (490 B.C.).

96. pelf : riches (generally with a bad meaning). Cp. Scott :

> ' Despite those titles, power, and pelf.'
> > (*Lay of the Last Minstrel*, Canto VI. i.).

100. whelm : overwhelm, engulf.

103. awful : inspiring awe—the correct use of the word. Cp. Dryden,
   Alexander's Feast :

> ' Aloft, in awful state,
>   The godlike hero sate ' ;

and Tennyson, *The Vision of Sin* :

> ' God made Himself an awful rose of dawn '

Milton, *Hymn on Christ's Nativity*, uses it in a still more literal
sense = full of awe :

> ' And kings sat still with awful eye,
>   As if they knew their sovran Lord was by.'

106. Akropolis : the steep, flat-topped rock, about 150 feet high (500
   feet above sea-level), around which the city of Athens grew up.

109-110. The distance from Marathon to Athens is over twenty-two miles
   The feat of Pheidippides is commemorated in our own day by the

Marathon Race, instituted at the revival of the Olympic Games in 1896.

111. Rejoice, we conquer : a translation of the Greek motto of the poem.
120. for his meed : death, in a moment of victory, was his reward.

SAMUEL TAYLOR COLERIDGE (1772–1834)

THE RIME OF THE ANCIENT MARINER.

In 1798 was published the *Lyrical Ballads*, the joint work of Wordsworth and Coleridge, the outcome of their sojourn together on the Quantock Hills and of their conversations on poetry. ' The thought suggested itself,' says Coleridge, ' that a series of poems might be composed of two sorts. In the one, the incidents and agents were to be, in part at least, supernatural. . . . For the second class, subjects were to be chosen from ordinary life. In this idea originated the plan of the "Lyrical Ballads " ; in which it was agreed that my endeavours should be directed to persons and characters supernatural, or at least romantic. Mr. Wordsworth, on the other hand, was to propose to himself as his object, to give the charm of novelty to things of every day, and to excite a feeling analogous to the supernatural, by awakening the mind's attention from the lethargy of custom, and directing it to the loveliness and the wonders of the world before us.' In the second edition of the *Lyrical Ballads*, published in 1800, Wordsworth added his famous Preface, in which he formulated his theories of poetry and of poetic diction. The first version of ' The Ancyent Marinere,' with all its quaint spellings and archaisms, Coleridge contributed to the joint volume.

The metre is the common ballad measure, the normal stanza consisting of four lines, of which the second and fourth rime. Coleridge sometimes lengthens the stanza by adding a line between the normal third and fourth lines, and riming with the former, or by extending it to six lines, the sixth riming with the second and fourth. In one instance (l. 203) he extends it to nine lines, the rimes being *aabccbddb*.

3. glittering eye : suggests the ' uncanny ' influence of the Mariner on the three gallants. Even when his weird tale is told, his eye remains bright (l. 618).
11. loon : low fellow, rascal. A Dutch word.
12. eftsoons : Coleridge weaves into the magic of his verse many archaic words such as this, taken from the Romantic poets, more especially from Spenser. They tend to heighten the air of mystery that envelops the poem.

25. The ship was *southward* bound. Cp. this stanza with the first in
    Part II., where the sun rises on the right and the ship's course is
    consequently northward.
36. **minstrelsy :** collective, the band of minstrels.
55. **clifts :** for cliffs, so used by Spenser.
62. **swound :** swoon.
63. **Albatross :** the largest and most powerful of sea-birds, to be met
    with in the Southern Ocean. It is capable of long-sustained flight,
    and frequently circles round ships for great distances (cp. l. 68).
64. **thorough :** a metrical variant of ' through.'
76. **vespers nine :** for nine (a sacred number) successive evenings the
    albatross perched on the mast for rest at the time of evening
    prayer.
82. This is one of the incidents supplied by Wordsworth.
98. **uprist :** a deliberate archaism
106. **that silent sea :** the Pacific. The ship had rounded the Horn.
128. **The death-fires :** the phosphorescent lights often to be seen at sea,
     especially in the Tropics. They were supposed to be prophetic of
     death.
152. **wist :** past tense of O.E. ' witan,' to know. Cp. ' They wist not
     what had become of Him ' (N.T.).
  6. **Gramercy :** an interjection, expressing gratitude or astonishment
     (as here). Fr. *grand merci*.
177. **flecked :** spotted, streaked.
178. **Heaven's Mother :** the Virgin Mary.
184. **gossameres :** fine spider-like threads, to be seen in fine weather
     floating in the air or resting on bushes.
200. There is no twilight in the Tropics.
209. **clomb :** an archaic past tense, used by the Romantic poets.
227. The sea-sand may often be seen marvellously ' ribbed ' when the tide
     has ebbed.
231. *i.e.*, ' I who am talking to you am alive and no spirit.'
245. **or :** ere.
275. **elfish :** weird, mysterious.
297. **silly ;** frail, useless ; lit. happy (same word as Ger. *selig*.)
310. **anear :** an adverb.
312. **sere :** withered, burnt. Same word as ' sear.' Cp. Shakespeare
     Macbeth, V. iii. :

> ' I have lived long enough : my way of life
> Is fall'n into the sear, the yellow leaf.'

314. **fire-flags sheen :** bright lightning-flashes.
317. **wan :** pale, faint.

319. **sedge :** coarse grass found in swamps. When the wind agitates it
     a moaning sound is produced.
325. **jag :** a ragged notch.
362. **jargoning :** chattering, twittering. The word comes from Lat.
     garrire, to chatter, through Fr.
489. **holy rood :** the cross of Christ.
512. **shrieve :** same word as ' shrive,' to give absolution after hearing
     confession.
535. **ivy-tod :** ' tod ' by itself means ivy-bush.
623. **forlorn :** deprived, destitute ; usually=forsaken.